Fly-tying Illustrated
for
Nymphs and Lures

The Angling Times Book of the Severn
Ken Cope

Catching Salmon
Richard Waddington

The Complete Guide to Coarse Fishing
(new edition)
Alan Wrangles

The Complete Guide to Sea Angling
(new edition)
Alan Wrangles

The Complete Trout and Salmon Fisherman
Jack Thorndike (editor)

*Dick Walker's Angling:
Theories and Practice, Past, Present and to Come*
Richard Walker

Fishing: The Complete Book
Tre Tryckare and E. Cagner

Fly-Dressing
David Collyer

Gravel Pit Angling
Peter Stone

Match Fishing Our Way
Ken Giles and Clive Smith

The Shell Book of Angling
Richard Walker

Still-Water Angling
Richard Walker

Fly-tying Illustrated
for
Nymphs and Lures

Freddie Rice

Member of
Association of Professional Game Angling Instructors
(Fly-dressing)

Illustrations by the author

David & Charles:
Newton Abbot · London · North Pomfret (VT)

For Doris, to whom I owe so much

ISBN 0 7153 6952 0
Library of Congress Catalog Card Number 76-2150

© F. A. Rice 1976

First published 1976
Second impression 1979

Set in 10 on 11 Univers
Printed in Great Britain by
Biddles Ltd, Guildford Surrey
for David & Charles (Publishers) Limited
Brunel House Newton Abbot Devon

Published in the United States of America
by David & Charles Inc
North Pomfret Vermont 05053 USA

Contents

Flies

Let Nature guide thee; sometimes golden wire
The shining bellies of the fly require . . .
Each gaudy bird some slender tribute brings,
And lends the growing insect proper wings:
Silks of all colours must their aid impart,
And every fur promote the fisher's art . . .
So just the colours shine through every part,
That Nature seems to live again in Art.

John Gay

Introduction

There is no keener pleasure than catching a trout with a fly you have dressed yourself.

Experience over many years has taught me that, next to personal instruction, fly-dressing is best learned from a simple text coupled with clear, numbered illustrations. The success of my students confirms this.

There has been a tremendous upsurge of interest in fly fishing on the ever-increasing number of man-made waters now available, from which very many fish are taken with dressings simulating sub-surface food forms, generally referred to as nymphs, and with artificial lures.

In this book I present a selection of popular and successful dressings, using modern materials and up to date methods, which it is my earnest wish will provide pleasure in the tying and fish in the net.

Acknowledgements

My sincere thanks are due, not only to those whose patterns appear in these pages, but also to the authors mentioned in the bibliography, and to all fly dressers, past and present, who have added to the store of knowledge which has accrued to the benefit of us all and which is reflected in these pages.

Particularly, I am indebted to:

Richard Walker, foremost angling correspondent and an angler and fly dresser of considerable achievement, for introducing me to the art many, many years ago;

John Veniard, an authority on fly dressing and the relevant materials who contributed, in no small way, to my fly dressing education;

John C. Haines, the bearded wonder, a grand friend, fly fisherman and fly dresser of no mean achievement, who undertook the exacting task of checking the instructions and illustrations for the dressings, and to his wife, Freddy;

my students, whose questions and comments have given me a clear understanding of the problems faced by the less experienced;

last, but by no means least, my wife for her constant encouragement and patient help in assembling and setting out my ideas.

F. A. RICE

The Way to Success

HOOKS It is advisable to test every hook in the vice by 'pinging' it with the thumbnail before proceeding with the dressing, for there is real irritation in having the hook of a completed fly break at the bend or, as more often happens, at the barb, if it is unusually brittle or the barb has been too deeply cut. Better to find the fault in the beginning. The hook should not be inserted in the vice in such a way that the point protrudes, for that point is razor sharp and is almost sure to cut or fray your working silk and may also neatly sever or weaken materials being wound on. Care is also needed when using hooks with off-set points that the whole of the bend is not inserted, for this also may cause breakages.

WAX The application of solid wax to working silk should be made a regular habit. It will minimise rotting of the silk and will help the silk to adhere to the bare hook shank. For many, well waxed silk will be found to be sufficiently tacky for the fur to be dubbed on but for the less experienced liquid wax may be found more helpful when forming dubbed bodies. The quantity should not be overdone and it should be remembered that the mixture contains a drying agent. For this reason the dubbing material should be applied immediately after the silk has been waxed. The cap of the bottle should be replaced after use to prevent evaporation.

SECURITY There is nothing more infuriating than a fly which disintegrates after a few casts. To avoid apoplexy remember that each securing turn of working silk must do its work—keep the silk in tension whenever you use it to secure material. Even the initial layer of silk, which should be wound over a bare hook shank to provide a firm base for wings and so forth, should be applied firmly. The dressing may otherwise rotate on the shank with disastrous results. Where tinsels and lurex are used it is advantageous to keep these under tension and to apply a thin coat of varnish to the side which will be innermost when wound on. A light coat of varnish applied to the underbody before winding on herls, such as peacock or ostrich, and wools and the like for bodies, increases security.

RIBBING It will be recognised that, when a ribbing of tinsel, lurex, silk or hackle quill is applied to the body, it is best wound on in a reverse spiral to that of the body materials. If this is not done, the ribbing is not only likely to sink into the turns of body material but also will not provide the intended cross-wound security. One proof of fly-dressing competence will be found in the way the ribbing is laid on — neat, firm and regular spacing being the criterion.

VARNISH There is little more unsightly than a fly finished off with too liberal an application of varnish to the final whipping. If the fly has been built up correctly and secured with firm turns of working silk, the application of varnish should be limited to setting the final whipping only. This can be adequately provided for by a small globule of varnish picked out from the bottle on the point of the dubbing needle and carefully applied, any wound hackles being pulled away from the hook eye. Alternatively, use a hackle protector, a piece of flat tin, plastic or cardboard, half an inch wide and about three inches long in which a number of holes of varying size are made. It is placed over the hook eye before the varnish is applied and thus prevents hackles and so forth being daubed.

HAIR WINGS A number of the lure patterns described herein have hair wings. Before tying in, hold the hair by the natural tips in one hand and tap out any short hairs and under-fur with the other. These are not needed and only add unnecessary, undesirable bulk.

Remember that hair wings are normally required to sit on top of the hook shank and the 'loop' method of tying in, as illustrated in the Butcher dressing, will produce the desired result. In fact, the 'loop' method can be applied to any material which is to be secured on top of the shank. Unless firmly secured, hair will tend to pull out and scatter on casting the fly. The remedy is firm tension on the working silk, an appropriate number of close securing turns (one or two taken round the hair only) and an adequate, but not overdone, application of varnish or fly cement to the joint.

FINISHING THE FLY HEAD Those who have mastered the 'whip finish' will consider the exercise a simple one, but to those who have not, I strongly recommend it as the most efficient method so far devised to finish flies neatly and securely. It is easily learned with a little practice. However, there is a whip finish tool available which virtually does the job for you provided you possess the wherewithal to buy it and you follow the instructions provided. Do not let yourself get into the habit of finishing your works of art with a series of half-hitches. These are definitely not the most secure and usually produce a bulky, unsightly head to the fly. Remember there is a twofold benefit if you can not only please the fish but your own aesthetic sense as well!

FLY-TYING SESSIONS When beginning a session you will find it advantageous to produce a number of one pattern of fly rather than one each of a number of different patterns. I would advise that, having decided which patterns are required, at least four, but preferably six, of a pattern be produced before moving on to the next. There is good sense in this for you will find that repeating the same pattern brings about an improvement as each one is tied. This, in turn, brings confidence. To maintain fly-tying skill there should not be too long a lapse of time between sessions.

Hook sizes referred to in the dressings are all old (Redditch) scale.

Amber Nymph (Dr Bell)

Materials

Hook   Down eye, April to June size 10, then size 12
Working Silk   Amber yellow
Rear Body   Amber yellow seal's fur or floss for use April to
June, but orange thereafter
Front Body   Brown seal's fur or floss
Wing Cases   5 to 8 fibres of woodcock or similar
Legs   A dozen honey coloured hackle fibres

Tying Instructions

1 Tie in working silk behind eye and wind it in close turns to start of bend.

2 Select and tie in the woodcock fibres as shown.

3 Apply liquid wax sparingly to working silk and dub on the *amber yellow* seal fur.

4 Wind on the dubbed seal fur to just two-thirds of the way along hook shank. Leave working silk hanging. Strip unused amber seal fur from working silk.

5 Apply liquid wax to working silk again and dub on the *brown* seal fur.

6 Wind on the dubbed seal fur to just short of hook eye. Leave working silk hanging.

7 Pull the woodcock fibres down to the right.

8 Tie down woodcock fibres just short of hook eye. Trim surplus leaving room for operations 9 and 10.

9 Tear the honey coloured fibres from a hackle of appropriate size and tie these in as shown.

10 Add a whip finish and varnish the whip to complete the fly.

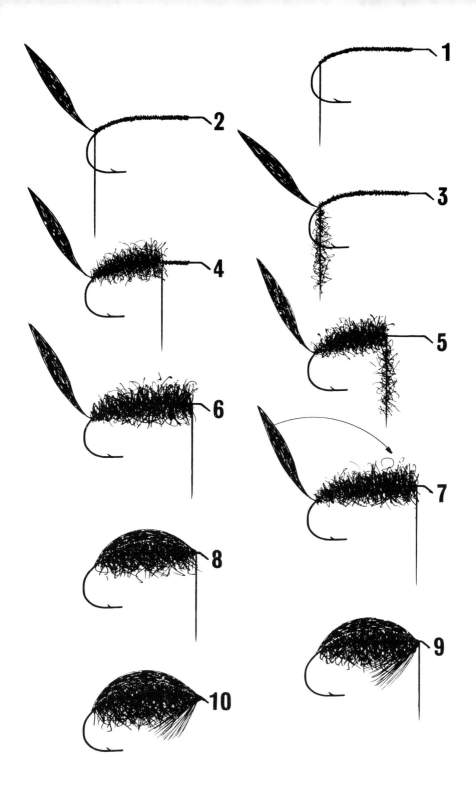

Bloodworm (Freddie Rice)

Materials
Hook   Down eye, size 12 or 10
Working Silk   Scarlet
Underbody   Scarlet lurex (red floss as substitute)
Body Wrap   Clear nylon 6lb breaking strain

Tying Instructions
1 Wind on working silk from behind eye to *well round* hook bend and tie in coloured lurex and nylon filament in that order.
2 Wind working silk back to just short of eye and leave hanging.
3 Wind on lurex flatly until working silk is reached. Tie off and remove surplus lurex.
4 Wind on clear nylon in close, even turns to eye. Tie off, add a whip finish and varnish the whip and whole body two coats.

Note
This fly, with a thin peacock or brown swan herl thorax, has also been found successful fished *slowly* in mid or upper water levels.

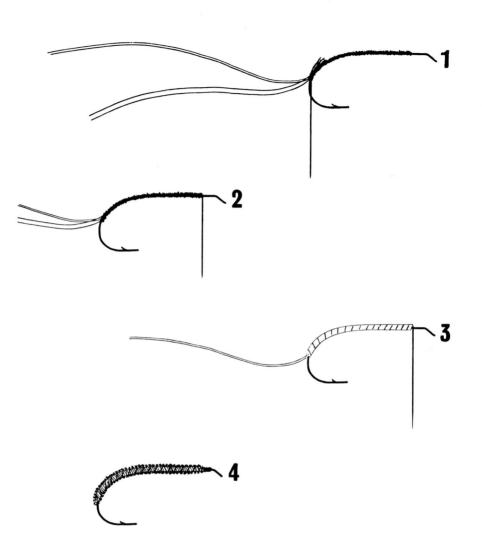

Bow Tie Buzzer (Frank Sawyer)

Materials

Hook   Down eye, size 12
Working Silk   None. Underbody wire used instead
Underbody   Gold coloured copper wire
Tails   Tips of pheasant tail fibres
Body   Silver tinsel (flat)
Overbody   4 or 5 red/brown cock pheasant tail fibres
'Bow Tie'   Small tuft of white nylon wool

Tying Instructions

1 Wind on gold coloured wire in close, *even* turns to start of hook bend. Leave wire hanging. (See note below.)

2 Using the wire, tie in tinsel at bend.

3 Wind on tinsel in touching turns to just short of eye and clip tinsel end in hackle pliers.

4 Using the wire at bend, tie in the cock pheasant tail fibres, fine points extending down and beyond bend.

5 Twist the pheasant tail fibres and the wire together to form a rope.

6 Wind on this rope so that the body tinsel shows through in neat, narrow bands. Tie off at eye with three *tight* turns of wire securing tinsel end and trim off surplus pheasant fibre ends, tinsel and wire at eye.

Using the fly   See illustrations 7, 8.
Frank Sawyer advocates that the nylon cast be fed *up* through the hook eye and a slip knot formed. A small tuft of white nylon wool is tightly enclosed in the knot formed and this is then pulled firmly up against the hook eye thus attaching the 'Bow Tie'.

Note

It seems some prefer to tie in the nylon wool at the very beginning of Operation No 1 as is shown in Illustration 1A.

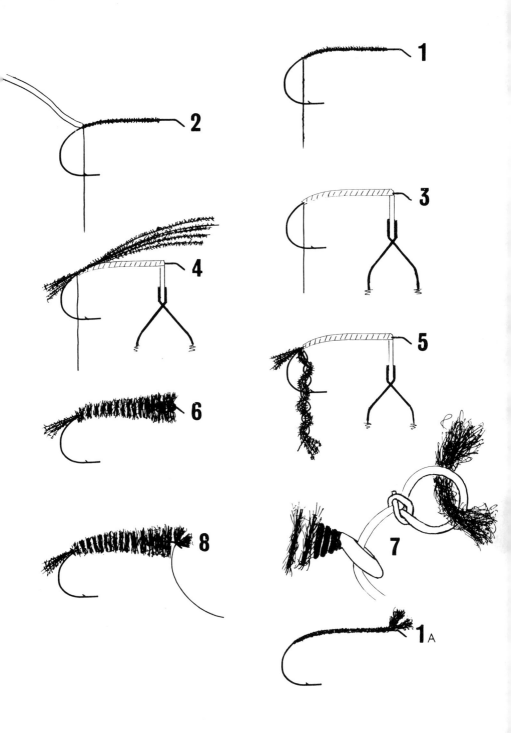

Brown Nymph (Tom Ivens)

Materials

Hook   Down eye, size 12, 10 or 8
Working Silk   Black or brown
Body   One strand darkish brown ostrich herl
Body Rib   Oval gold tinsel
Horns   Two strands STRIPPED green ostrich herl
Head   Two strands UNSTRIPPED bronze peacock herl

Tying Instructions

1 Wind on a few turns of working silk at bend and tie in two strands (stripped) of green ostrich herl, oval gold tinsel and one strand of brown ostrich herl (unstripped) in that order. The wind silk back to $\frac{3}{16}$ " from eye.

2 Wind on unstripped brown ostrich herl to form body. Tie off and remove surplus ostrich.

3 Wind on oval gold tinsel in open turns. Tie off and remove surplus tinsel.

4 Bring horns (stripped herls) directly over body and tie down at head *leaving* herl ends protruding over eye.

5 Tie in two strands of natural peacock herl.

6 Wind on peacock herl (twisted) forming head. Tie off and remove surplus peacock herl.

7 Bend the horns back and separate them over the body. Tie down, maintaining separation. Add a whip finish and varnish the whip.

Note

See page 44 for method of stripping 'flue' from ostrich and peacock herls.

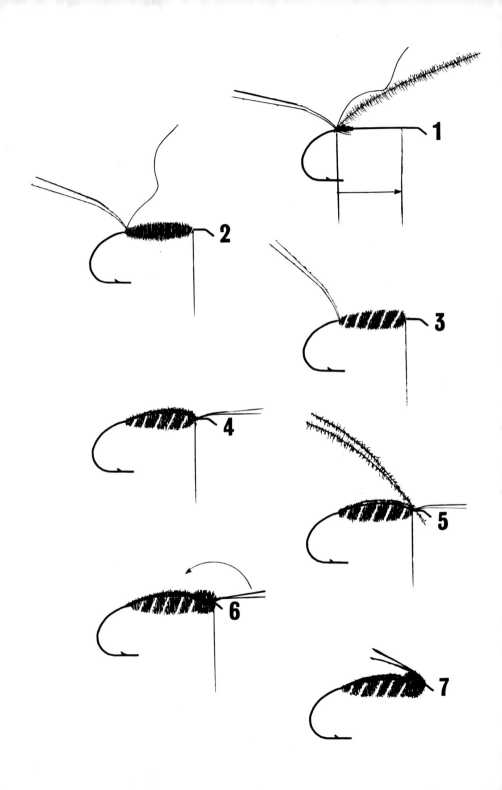

Brown and Green Nymph (Tom Ivens)

Materials
Hook   Down eye, size 10 or 8
Working Silk   Brown
Tails, Overbody and Head   Four natural peacock herls
Body   One each of olive and brown dyed ostrich herls
Body Rib   Oval gold tinsel

Tying Instructions
1 Wind on a few turns of working silk at start of bend. Tie in peacock herls (leaving ¼'' extending as tails), tinsel, and the olive and brown ostrich herls. Then wind working silk back to ⅛'' from eye. If lead is needed wind on lead wire now.

2 Varnish body and whilst still wet wind on olive and brown ostrich herls *together* to form body of alternate colours. Tie off at head — remove surplus herl ends.

3 Wind on tinsel in open turns and tie off at eye. Remove surplus tinsel.

4 Bring the peacock herls over the body to head and tie down. **Do not trim surplus peacock herl.**

5 Twist the peacock herls together at eye end and wind these on to form a bold head. Tie off, trim any surplus, add a whip finish and varnish the whip.

Note
Whilst producing a useful nymph form, this fly has a fish-like silhouette and 'stripping through' has paid dividends, particularly when leaded or used unleaded with a sinking line.

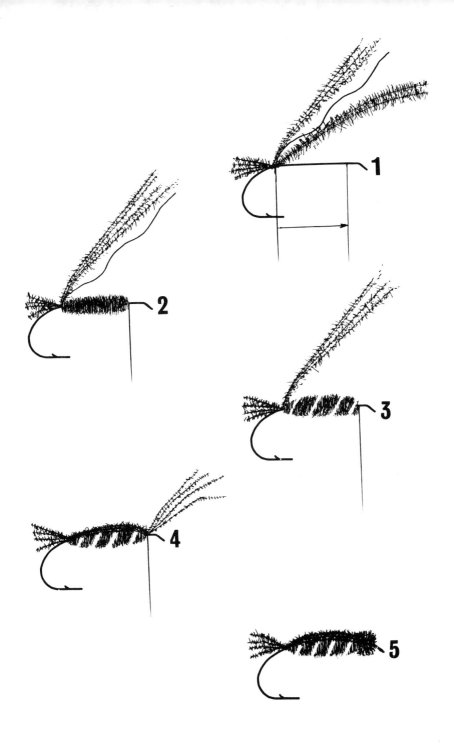

Chompers (Richard Walker)

Materials
Hook   Down eye, size 14, 12 or 10, to match insect intended
Working Silk   See colour list below
Body   Four herls as list of body materials below
Shell Back   Brown speckled turkey fibres or coloured
'Raffene' — see list below

Tying Instructions
1 Wind on a few turns of working silk at start of bend and tie in the shell back (extended just short of eye) and body materials in that order.
2 Wind working silk to ⅛'' from hook eye in close turns.
3 Varnish the turns of working silk.
4 Whilst the varnish *is still wet* twist the body material (ostrich or peacock herls) into a rope.
5 Wind this rope round hook shank in close turns to ⅛'' from hook eye. Tie off and trim surplus herl.
6 Pull the shell back material down and forward *tightly* to just behind hook eye and tie this down securely. Trim surplus.
7 Add a whip finish and varnish the whip.

Note
Raffene must be well wet before tying in. Hook size should match the natural insect that the colour combination suggests, adding fine copper wire or lead under body material if desired.

'Raffene' Colours	Body Material	Working Silk	Fly Produced
Clear	Golden yellow ostrich	Black	General representative
Brown	Olive ostrich	Olive	ditto
Pale buff	Buff ostrich	Brown	Shrimp
Pea green	White ostrich	Olive	Small Corixa
Black	Peacock	Black	Beetle
Speckled turkey	Golden yellow ostrich	Black	General representative
Speckled turkey	White ostrich	Olive	Large Corixa

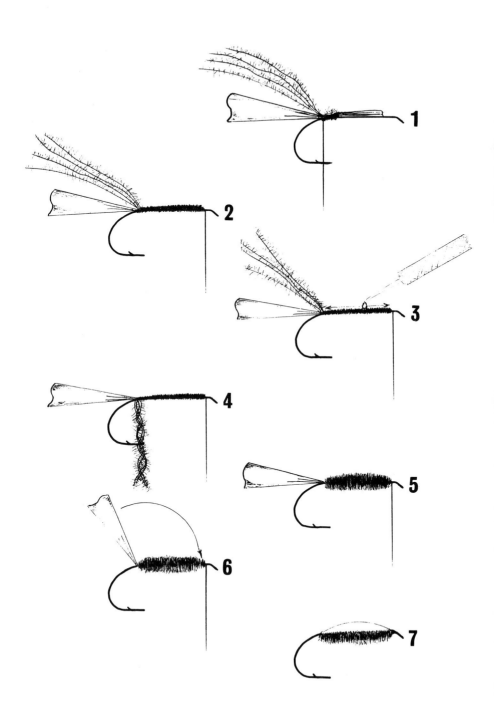

Corixa (Freddie Rice)
(Lesser Water Boatman)

Materials
Hook   Down eye, size 14 or 12
Working Silk   Brown
Tag   Oval silver tinsel
Body   Pale buff wool or floss silk
Wing Cases   Black (or dark brown) Raffene well damped
Oars   Buff condor, two fibres each folded in two

Tying Instructions
1   Wind on a few turns of working silk at start of hook bend and tie in tinsel. Then wind silk to right for $\frac{1}{16}$''.

2   Wind on tinsel to form tag (4 turns). Tie off and remove surplus.

3   Tie in Raffene strip and wool. Then wind working silk to the right to cover one-third of hook shank.

4   Wind on the wool back and forth to form body ending where silk hangs. *Do not* trim surplus wool.

5   Fold and flatten condor in two and tie in one folded strip on each side of body as shown to point diagonally outwards.

6   Wind on wool for remaining two-thirds of body. Tie off and trim surplus wool.

7A Pull Raffene strip tightly forward over body to eye

7B and tie down. Trim surplus Raffene. Add a whip finish and varnish the whip.

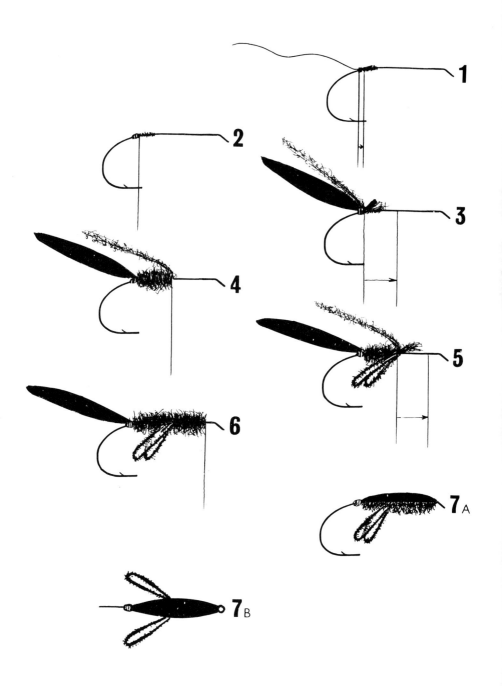

Damsel Nymph (Freddie Rice)

Materials

Hook   Long shank, down eye, size 12
Working Silk   Olive
Tails   4 to 6 Olive hackle fibres — tips trimmed square
Body   Olive marabou silk
Body Rib   Fine gold wire
Thorax   Olive seal fur
Legs   Olive beard hackle well spread out, or brown partridge

Tying Instructions

1 Wind on working silk in close turns from ⅛'' from eye to start of bend. Tie in gold wire, tail and a length of marabou silk. Then wind working silk two-thirds along hook shank.

2 Wind on marabou silk to form a slightly tapered body until working silk is reached. Tie off two turns and remove surplus marabou.

3 Wind on gold wire tightly in an *open spiral.* Tie off at end of body and remove surplus wire.

4 Apply liquid wax sparingly to working silk and dub on the olive seal fur.

5 Wind on dubbed fur thickening to represent thorax. Tie off leaving room for operation 6.

6 Turn fly upside down in vice. Select and strip out 6 to 8 fibres from a brown partridge hackle and take one turn round these and hook shank. Leave silk hanging and, pressing with the thumb or forefinger, splay out the fibres as shown in 6A and 6B. Then, keeping the fibres splayed, secure them in that position with two or three turns of working silk. Complete winding of head and add a whip finish which should be varnished.

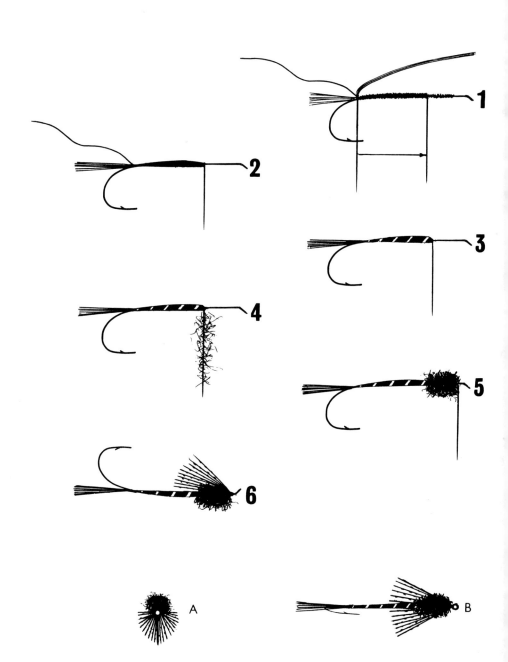

Floating Snail (Cliff Henry)

Materials

Hook   Down eye, wide gape, size 14, 12 or 10
Working Silk   Black
Body   Shaped cork (or Plastazote)
Body Cover   Stripped peacock eye quill
Front Body Edge   Unstripped natural peacock herl

Tying Instructions

A Cut and shape the cork with a razor blade or sharp knife.

B Then *partly* slit one side to accommodate hook shank.

1 Wind on a turn or two of working silk at bend and tie in the *stripped* peacock quill.

2 Pass the slit cork body over the hook shank. (Some people line the slit with 'Araldite'. Let it dry.) Bind the cork body lightly to the hook shank with working silk leaving the silk hanging just short of the flat front cork edge behind eye.

3 Wind the *stripped* peacock quill round the cork body progressing towards the flat front. Tie off with working silk at front cork edge and remove any surplus stripped quill.

4 Tie in one strand of *unstripped* bronze (natural) peacock herl near flat front edge of cork body.

5 Wind on the *unstripped* peacock herl at front edge of body for two turns only. Tie off with working silk, remove surplus herl, carry working silk to hook just behind eye and add a whip finish. Varnish the whip.

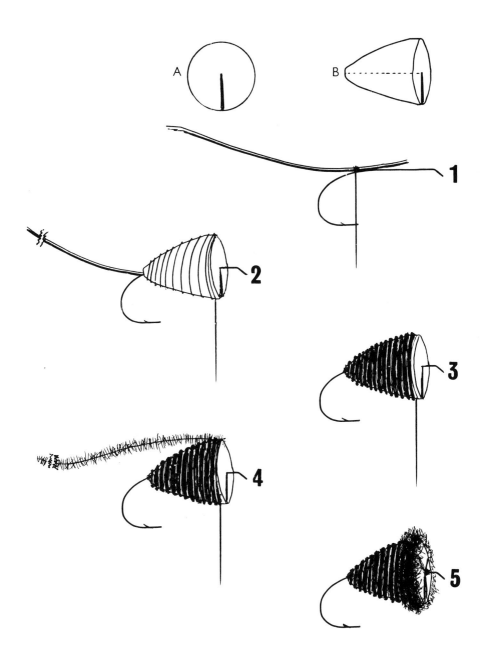

A

B

1

2

3

4

5

Fuzza Buzza (John Haines)

Materials

Hook   Down eye, normal or long shank, size 12 or 10
Working Silk   Black
Underbody Weight   Fine lead or copper wire
Body   Black seal fur wound on thinly
Body Rib   Silver or gold wire
Thorax   Two natural peacock herls

Tying Instructions

1 Wind on fine lead wire from ⅛" from eye to start of bend. Then wind on a few turns of working silk part way round the hook bend and tie in the wire rib.

2 Apply liquid wax sparingly to working silk and dub on seal fur.

3 Wind on seal fur three-quarters of shank length. Leave silk hanging.

4 Wind on wire rib in open turns to where silk hangs. Tie off and remove surplus wire.

5 Tie in the peacock herls. Then wind working silk to just behind eye.

6 Wind on peacock herls to form a bold thorax. Tie off and remove surplus herl.

7 Finish winding head, add a whip finish and varnish the whip.

Note

If you wish to fish this fly near or at the surface, omit the underbody weight.

Bodies of fiery brown or olive green seal fur are also successful. Method of tying is unaltered.

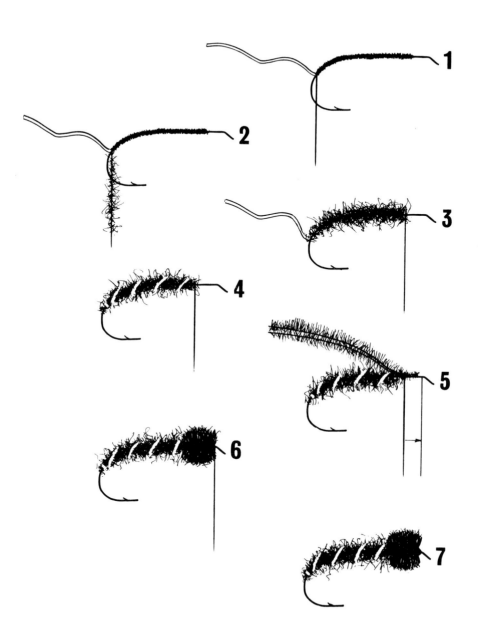

Gold Ribbed Hare's Ear (G.R.H.E.)

Materials

Hook   Down eye, size 16 or 14
Working Silk   Primrose
Tails   Four longish hairs from hare's ear
Body   Hare's fur dubbed on to working silk, ear fur nearest
bend, longer darker fur fibres from hare's body nearest eye
of hook
Body Rib   Oval gold tinsel or fine flat gold tinsel

Tying Instructions

1 Tie in working silk behind hook eye and then wind it in close turns to start of bend. At that point, tie in the four tail fibres (natural points extending approximately ⅛'' beyond bend) and the oval gold tinsel.

2 Preferably pick or, alternatively, cut the fur from the ear and, after applying liquid wax sparingly to the working silk, dub the hare's fur, *not too thickly*, on to the waxed silk.

3 Wind on dubbed fur. A second dubbing of fur may well be necessary to complete the fly and this should include some of the longer darker hairs. Tie off behind eye.

4 Wind on the tinsel tightly in open turns to eye and tie off. Remove surplus tinsel, add a whip finish and varnish the whip.

5 Using a dubbing needle, or similar instrument, pick out a few of the longer hairs at eye end.

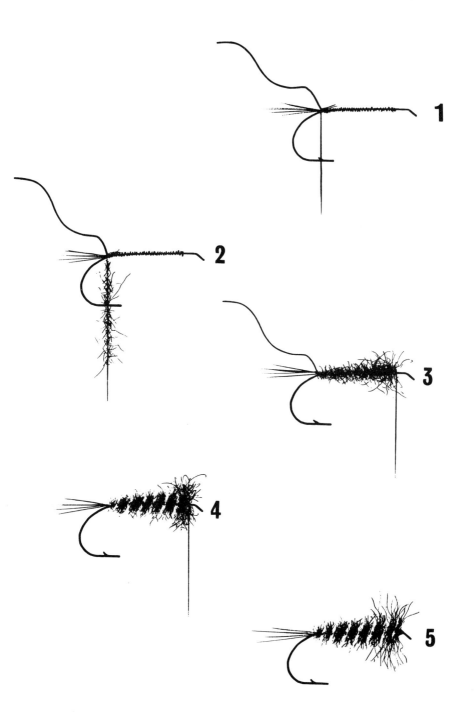

Green Nymph (Tom Ivens)

Materials
Hook   Down eye, size 12, 10 or 8
Working Silk   Green
Underbody   White floss
Body   Pale green nylon monofilament
Hackle   Brown partridge
Head   Two strands bronze peacock herl

Tying Instructions
1 Wind on a few turns of working silk at start of hook bend. Tie in green nylon (notch the end with your teeth) and white floss. Then wind working silk back to a good ⅛" from eye.

2 Wind on floss underbody, thickening slightly for thorax, and tie off. Remove surplus floss.

3 Wind on nylon in close turns until working silk is reached. Tie off and remove surplus nylon. Varnish body.

4 Select and tie in a brown partridge breast hackle behind eye.

5 Wind on partridge hackle, two turns only, and tie off. Remove surplus hackle ends.

6 Tie in two strands of bronze peacock herl at eye.

7 Pull the partridge fibres towards the hook bend to prevent them being caught up, then twist the peacock herls together and wind on about four turns to form the head. Tie off, remove surplus herl, add a whip finish and varnish the whip.

Note
Use nylon .009 for size 12 hooks, increasing to .014 for size 8 hooks.

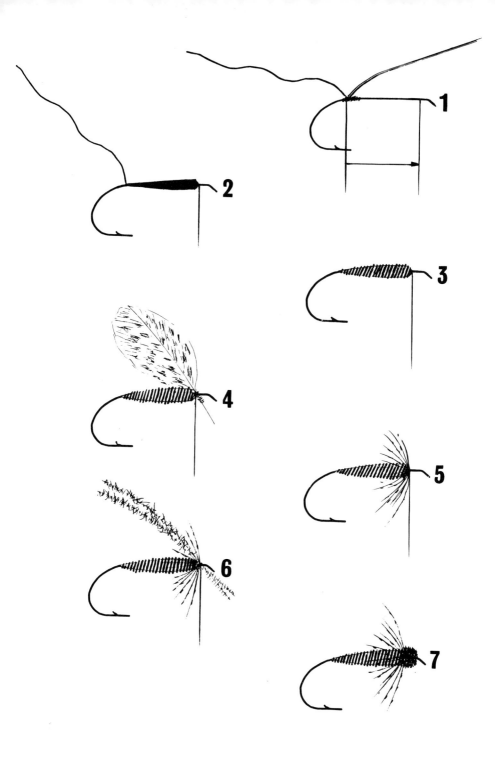

Green and Yellow Nymph (Tom Ivens)

Materials
Hook   Down eye, size 12 or 10
Working Silk   Green or black
Rear Body   Two strands green dyed swan herl
Front Body   Two strands deep yellow dyed swan herl
Head   Two strands peacock herl

Tying Instructions
1 Wind on a few turns of working silk at start of bend and tie in the two green swan herls. Then wind working silk to halfway along hook shank.

2 Wind on green herls until the silk is reached. Tie off and remove surplus herl.

3 Where the green herl ends, tie in the two deep yellow swan herls. Then wind working silk to ⅛'' from eye.

4 Starting close up to the end of the green herl, wind on the yellow herls until the working silk is reached behind eye. Tie off and remove surplus herl.

5 Tie in the two strands of peacock herl.

6 Wind on peacock herls to form a largish head. Wind silk through head and tie off. Add a whip finish and varnish the whip.

Note
Some swan herl is too garish a green for this fly—an olive-green is preferable.

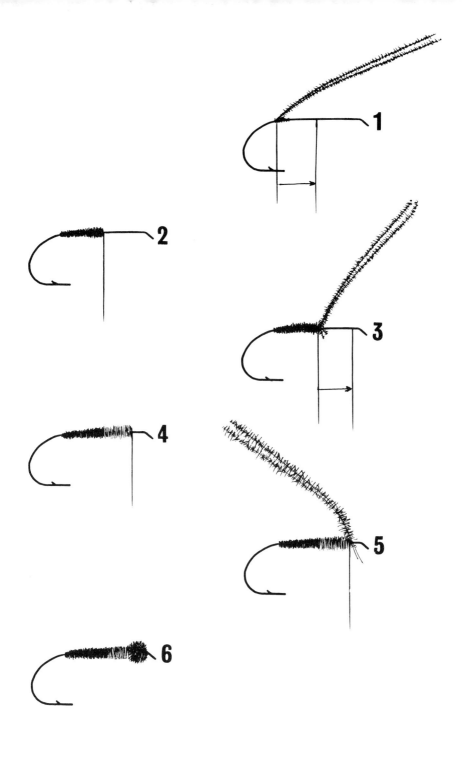

Hatching Midge Pupa (John Goddard)

Materials

Hook   Straight eye, round bend, size 14, 12 or 10
Working Silk   Same as chosen body colour
Tail Tag   White glass fibres or white hackle fibres
Body   Black, brown, red or green marabou silk
Body Rib   Red pattern, wide silver lurex
  Other patterns, narrow silver lurex
Body Cover   P.V.C.   " to ⅛" wide
Thorax   Either green peacock or buff condor herl
Head Filaments   As tail tag

Tying Instructions

1 Wind on a turn or two of working silk well round bend and tie in tail tag fibres (to point diagonally down), the P.V.C., lurex and marabou silk in that order. Then wind working silk to a point three-quarters along shank.

2 Wind on marabou silk (flat) for body and tie off when working silk is reached. Remove excess marabou silk.

3 Wind on tinsel in an open spiral and tie off (for red pattern leave only narrow bands of red showing). Remove excess lurex.

4 Wind on P.V.C. to cover body and tie off. Remove excess P.V.C.

5 Tie in three peacock *or* condor herls at eye end of the body and the head filaments to project just beyond hook eye.

6 Wind working silk over filaments and hook shank to just short of eye.

7 Wind on the herls to form thorax and tie off. Lift head filaments and take a few turns of working silk diagonally *round hook shank only* to keep head filaments lifted. Add a whip finish and varnish the whip keeping filaments up and clear of varnish.

Note

With the red pattern only, a hot orange pad on top of the thorax is often included to represent the wing cases of the pupa this dressing represents.

38

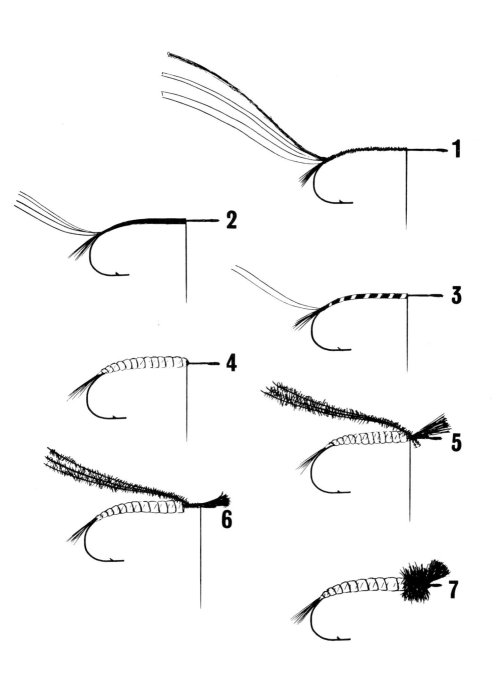

Killer Bug (Frank Sawyer)

Materials

Hook   Down eye, size 12, 11, 10 or 9
Working Silk   None, underbody wire used instead
Underbody   Red/bronze copper wire as thick as hook shank
Body   Chadwicks no 477 wool (fawn/buff)

Tying Instructions

1 Starting behind eye, wind on copper wire to bend in close turns and then back to just behind eye.

2 Use the wire to tie in a length of specified wool securely at eye.

3 Having done this, wind the wire back tightly to start of hook bend. Leave wire hanging.

4 Wind on the wool in close turns to start of hook bend, then back to just short of eye, and then once again back to start of hook bend forming shape with the triple layer of wool. Secure end of wool with wire using two or three *tight* turns.

5 Trim off surplus wire and wool neatly, pressing the wire 'point' into the body so that it cannot be felt.

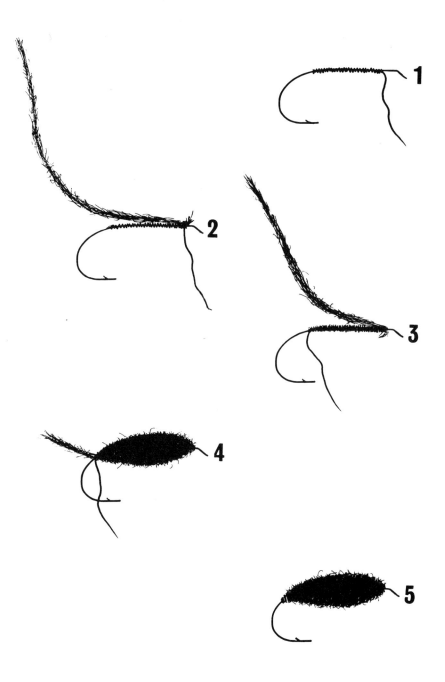

Mayfly Nymph (Freddie Rice)

Materials

Hook   Down eye, long shank, fine wire, size 10
Working Silk   Olive
Tail and Wing Cases   Three cock pheasant centre tail fibres
Body   Brown and olive seal's fur, mixed — thickened over last
  one-third of body behind eye
Body Rib   Gold wire
Legs   Brown partridge

Tying Instructions

1 Spiral working silk from behind eye to start of bend and tie in
  the cock pheasant tail fibres — natural points extending ⅜''
  beyond bend — and the gold wire.

2 Mix the brown and olive seal fur and, after applying liquid
  wax sparingly to working silk, dub the fur on to the silk.

3 Wind on the seal fur, covering the cock pheasant fibres to
  form a tapered body two-thirds of shank length. Leave
  pheasant fibres projecting upwards.

4 Dub on additional mixed seal fur.

5 Pull the projecting pheasant fibres towards hook bend and
  wind on seal fur to form a thickened thorax. Tie off.

6 Wind on the gold wire in open turns to behind eye. Tie off
  and remove surplus wire.

7 Pull cock pheasant fibres forward over thorax to eye and tie
  down. Remove surplus pheasant fibre ends.

8 Turn fly upside down in vice. Tear out a small bunch of
  brown partridge fibres and tie these in as for a beard hackle
  but slightly splayed out. Trim surplus partridge fibre ends.

9 Build up a head, add a whip finish and varnish the whip.

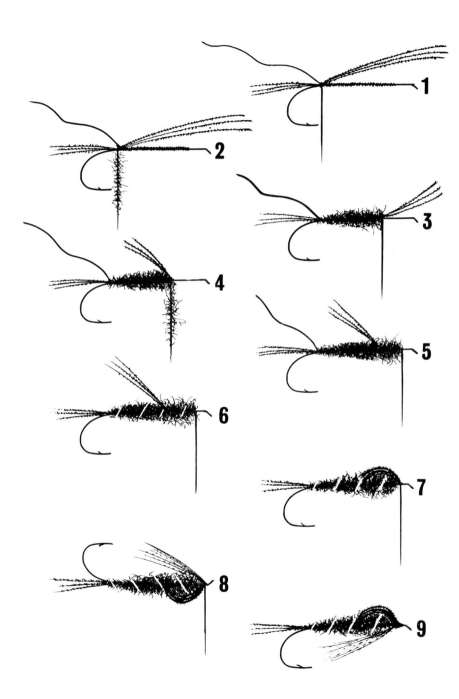

Mosquito or Grey Midge Pupa
(Dave Collyer)

Materials
Hook   Down eye, size 12
Working Silk   Black
Body   Stripped quill from 'eye' of peacock feather
Thorax   Dubbed mole fur

Tying Instructions

1 Tie in working silk ⅛'' from eye and then wind it in close turns to well round the hook bend. At that point tie in the fine point of the stripped quill taken from the 'eye' portion of a peacock feather.

2 Wind the working silk back in close turns to ⅛'' from hook eye.

3 Wind on the stripped quill in close turns to form a segmented body and tie off ⅛'' from eye.

4 Apply liquid wax sparingly to the working silk and prepare the mole or similar fur 'pinched' or cut from the skin, ready for winding on.

5 Wind on the dubbed fur just behind the hook eye to form thorax which should result in a pronounced round ball. Tie off, add a neat whip finish and varnish the whip, keeping it away from the thorax fur.

Note
An easy way of 'stripping' peacock quills is to erase the 'flue' with a rubber eraser. Others feel it is as easy to use the thumb nail as a scraper. The quill is necessary from the 'eye' of the feather as this usually provides a quill having light and dark edges, thus improving the segmented body appearance.

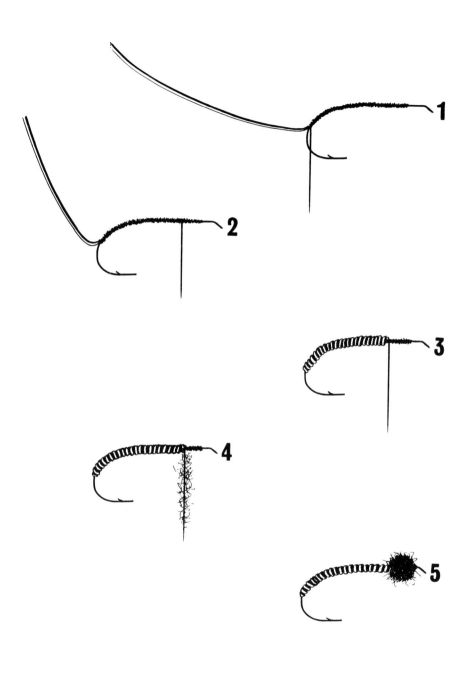

Olive Nymph (Freddie Rice)
(General Representative Pattern)

Materials
Hook   Down eye, size 10 or long shank, size 12
Working Silk   Olive
Tail   Fine tips of body material
Body   Three buff condor primary fibres coloured medium-olive
Thorax   Dark olive seal fur, a few hairs being picked out
Wing Cases   Thick ends of body material laid over thorax

Tying Instructions
1 Wind on a few turns of working silk at bend then tie in three condor fibres with fine points extending beyond bend for ⅛" to $\frac{3}{16}$" — no more.

2 Pull the longer condor fibres to the left and wind working silk in close turns for two-thirds length of hook shank and leave it hanging there.

3 Wind on the long condor fibres in close turns thickening slightly towards point where silk hangs. *Do not remove* excess condor ends.

4 Apply liquid wax sparingly to working silk and whilst still tacky dub on the dark olive seal fur, not too thickly.

5 Pull the condor out of the way to the left and wind on the seal fur already on the working silk, building up a thorax hump. Leave silk hanging behind eye.

6 Pull the condor ends forward over thorax to eye and tie these down. Trim any surplus condor left.

7 Build up a neat head, add a whip finish and varnish the whip. Then, with a dubbing needle or similar, pick out several of the longer hairs of seal fur.

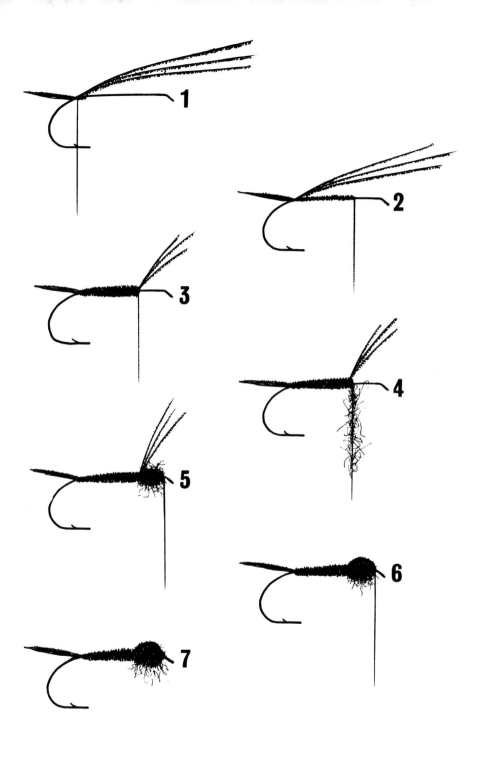

Olive Sun Nymph (Richard Aylott)

Materials
Hook   Down eye, size 14 or 12
Working Silk   Pale green
Tail   Small golden pheasant topping
Body   Greenish-yellow fluorescent floss
Body Rib   Fine gold thread
Head   Two natural bronze peacock herls

Tying Instructions
1 Wind on a few turns of working silk at start of hook bend and tie in the golden pheasant topping (fibres upward), gold thread and fluorescent floss, in that order. Then wind working silk back to approximately ⅛" from eye.

2 Wind on fluorescent floss to form a very slim body. Tie off where shown and trim surplus floss.

3 Wind on gold thread tightly in open turns. Tie off and remove surplus gold thread.

4 Tie in two natural bronze peacock herls at eye end of body.

5 Wind on the peacock herls two to four turns to form a neat head. Tie off, trim surplus herl, add a whip finish and varnish the whip.

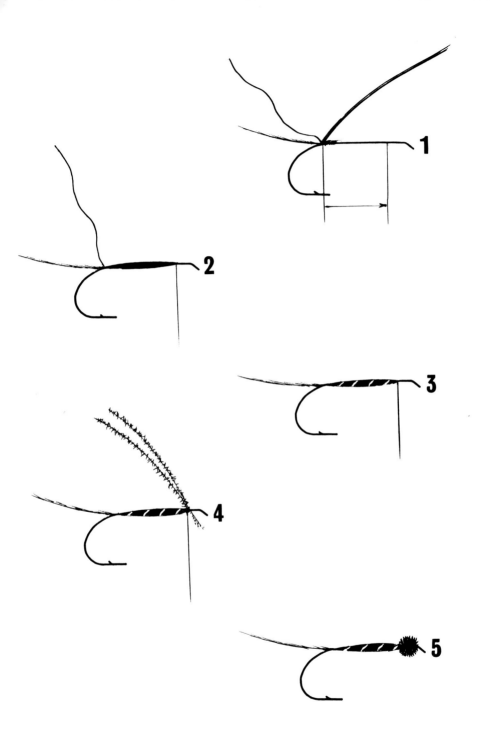

Phantom Pupa (John Goddard)

Materials

Hook   Down eye, size 16
Working Silk   Brown
Body   One strand only of white marabou silk
Body Rib   Fine silver lurex
Thorax   Two strands only of orange marabou silk
Overlay   Clear P.V.C. $\frac{1}{16}$" wide, wound over body and thorax

Tying Instructions

1 Wind on a few turns of working silk at start of bend and tie in P.V.C. strip, lurex and white marabou silk in that order. Then wind working silk three-quarters of the way towards eye.

2 Wind on white floss flatly to form a slim body. Tie off and remove surplus floss.

3 Wind on lurex in open turns and tie off. Remove surplus lurex.

4 Tie in orange marabou silk at eye end of body.

5 Wind working silk to just behind hook eye.

6 Wind on orange marabou silk to form thorax, stopping just before eye.

7 Wind on P.V.C. strip tightly over both body and thorax. Tie off, remove surplus P.V.C., add a whip finish and varnish the whip.

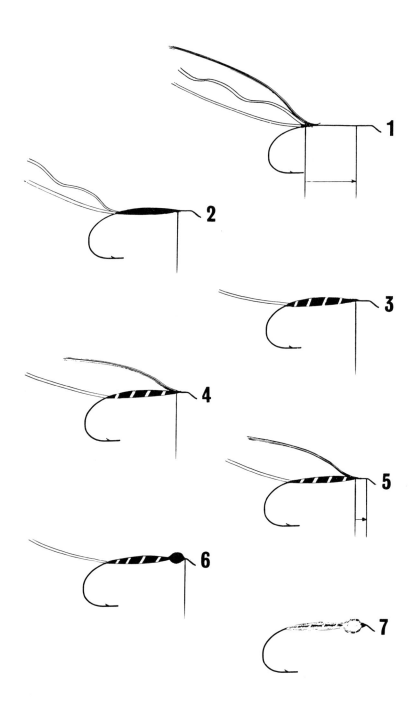

Pheasant Tail Nymph (Frank Sawyer)

Materials
Hook   Down eye, size 15 or 14
Working Silk   None, body wire used instead
Body   Fine red-bronze copper wire
Tails, Overbody and Thorax   Four browny-red cock pheasant
  tail fibres, the longer the better

Tying Instructions
1 Wind on copper wire in tight touching turns from start of hook bend to just before eye. Then form the hump for the thorax and thence back to start of bend. The wire must not be able to rotate on the hook shank.

2 Select the four cock pheasant tail fibres and tie these in, using wire, so that the natural tips stand out about ⅛" beyond hook bend and are splayed out.

3 Twist the longer pheasant tail fibres round the wire as reinforcement.

4 Wind tail fibres and wire twisted together over wire body back to eye. Then separate pheasant tail fibres from the wire but *do not* trim either the fibres or wire.

5 Wind copper wire back to bend side of thorax. The separated pheasant fibres projecting over eye are then ready for operation 6.

6 Pull pheasant tail fibres *to rear* of thorax hump and tie down using the copper wire. Then wind the copper wire back over thorax to eye in *open* turns.

7 Pull pheasant tail fibres *forward* over thorax hump and tie them down behind eye using the copper wire. Finish with three or four *tight* turns of wire at eye in place of the usual whip finish. Trim excess wire.

8 Finished fly appears thus.

Note
It is a feature of this fly that the copper wire colouring should show in places.

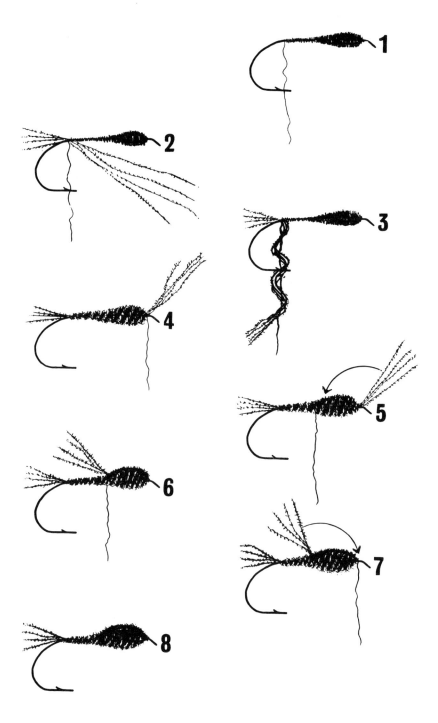

P.V.C. Nymph (John Goddard)

Materials

Hook   Down eye, size 16, 14 or 12
Working Silk   Yellow
Tails   Olive condor herls—three
Underbody   Copper wire
Rear Body   Silver lurex
Rear Body Cover   Olive dyed P.V.C. $\frac{1}{16}$ '' wide
Front Body   Olive condor
Thorax   Blackish pheasant tail fibres—three

Tying Instructions

1 Starting at bend cover hook shank with copper wire building up a hump to represent thorax where shown. Finish with three tight turns. Remove excess wire. (Regulate sinking rate by varying amount of copper wire used.)

2 Wind on working silk at bend, then tie in the three condor herls (with tips protruding beyond bend), the silver lurex and P.V.C. strip. Then wind working silk back to eye.

3 Wind on condor herls over whole and tie in at eye. Remove waste herl. Then wind working silk back to bend side of thorax.

4 Wind on lurex in open turns to start of thorax and tie off. Remove surplus lurex.

5 Wind P.V.C. tightly over body to start of thorax. Tie off and remove surplus P.V.C. Then wind working silk to eye.

6 Select and tie in the pheasant tail fibres. Then wind silk back to just behind thorax.

7 Pull pheasant tail fibres down and just to the rear of thorax and tie down. Then wind working silk back to eye.

8 Pull pheasant tail fibres forward once again over thorax to eye and tie down.

9 Remove surplus pheasant tail fibres. Add a whip finish and varnish the whip.

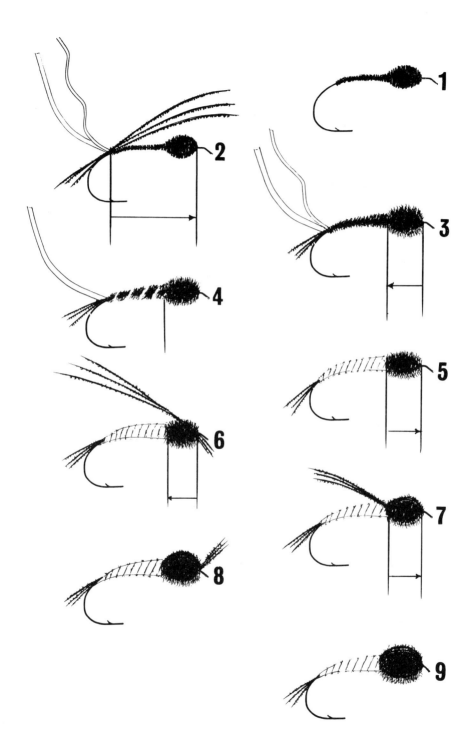

Sedge Pupa (John Goddard)

Materials

Hook   Long shank, wide gape, size 12 or 10
Working Silk   Brown
*Body   Cream, dark brown, orange or olive seal's fur The two
latter colours can be lightly covered with fluorescent floss of
the same colour*
Body Rib   Fine silver lurex
Thorax   Dark brown condor herls — three
Wing Cases   Light brown condor herls — four
Head Hackle   Honey or rusty hen — two turns only

Tying Instructions

1 Wind on a few turns of working silk at start of bend and, if
fluorescent floss is to be incorporated, tie it in now,
together with silver lurex.

2 Using liquid wax, dub selected colour of seal fur on to
working silk.

3 Wind on dubbed seal fur three-quarters of the length of hook
shank. Leave silk hanging. (If fluorescent floss is used wind
it on *lightly* over seal fur now and tie off with working silk.
Not shown in illustration.)

4 Wind on lurex in open turns to point shown and tie off with
working silk. Tie in four strands of light condor and three
strands of dark condor. Then wind working silk back to ⅛''
from eye.

5 Wind on dark condor to form hump for thorax and tie off.
Remove excess.

6 Pull light condor down over thorax *to eye* and tie down.
Then wind silk back to rear of thorax by an *open* turn.

7 Pull light condor over thorax *to rear* and tie down. Then
wind silk back to eye by an *open* turn.

8 Pull light condor forward once again over thorax and tie
down. Remove surplus. Then tie in the honey or rusty hen
hackle.

9 Wind on hackle two turns only and tie off. Remove surplus
hackle, add a whip finish and varnish the whip.

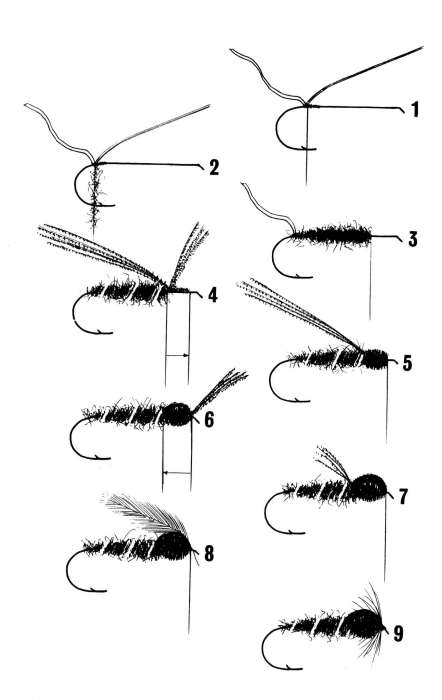

'Sooper Dooper Pooper' (Richard Walker) (Chironomid Pupa)

Materials

Hook   Down eye, as listed
Working Silk   As appropriate to the colour combination
chosen
Head and Tail   Long fibres stripped from a white hackle
Abdomen   Swan, goose, condor or other primary fibres, as list
Abdomen Rib   The stripped white hackle stalk or as list
Thorax   Peacock herls (2 or 3) or brown feather fibres, as list

Tying Instructions

1 Secure a few turns of working silk to hook behind eye and lay the white hackle fibres horizontally over hook shank — fine points to bend — so that they overhang at both eye and bend.

2 Wind working silk over both hackle fibres and shank in close turns until approximately one-third round hook bend.

3 At that point, tie in abdomen rib and abdomen feather fibres both by their fine points and in that order.

4 Wind working silk back in close turns to point shown in Drawing 4 and then varnish the turns of silk.

5 Twist the abdomen fibres into a rope.

6 Whilst the varnish is *still wet,* wind on this rope in close turns *clockwise to shank,* tying off when working silk is reached. Then trim surplus fibres.

7 Wind on the selected ribbing material in an open spiral *anti-clockwise to shank.* Tie off when working silk is reached and trim surplus ribbing.

8 Tie in specified thorax material at eye end of abdomen. Then wind working silk in close turns to just short of eye. Varnish those turns of silk.

9 Whilst the varnish is *still wet,* twist the thorax material into a rope and wind this on in close turns to form a bold thorax leaving room to tie off, then trim, add a whip finish *on the eye side* of white fibres and varnish the whip.

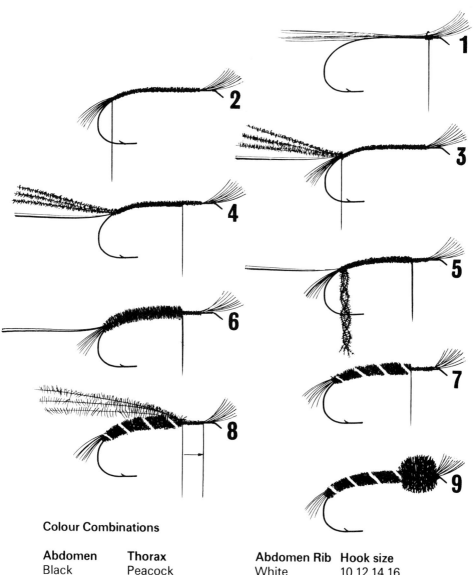

Colour Combinations

Abdomen	Thorax	Abdomen Rib	Hook size
Black	Peacock	White	10 12 14 16
Claret	Peacock	White	10 12
Red	Peacock	White	12
Green	Peacock	White	12 16
Brown olive	Brown feather fibre	White	12
Golden olive	Peacock	Gold lurex	12 14
Green olive	Peacock	Crimson	8

The Shrimper (John Goddard)

Materials
Hook   Down eye Limerick, size 14, 12 or 10
Working Silk   Orange
Underbody   Copper wire
Body   Olive marabou silk
Body Rib   Orange fluorescent silk
Upper Body Cover   P.V.C. widest at centre, but
   approximately ⅛"
Palmer Hackle   Honey

Tying Instructions
1 Wind on the copper wire from eye to bend, thickening in the middle to form hump, finishing with two tight turns. Trim surplus wire.

2 Wind on a few turns of working silk at bend then tie in shaped P.V.C., hackle and marabou silk in that order. If tying fly to show mating colour for June and July also tie in fluorescent silk after hackle. Then wind working silk to ⅛" from eye.

3 Wind on marabou silk to cover copper underbody and tie off ⅛" from eye. Remove surplus marabou. (*For mating type only*, wind on fluorescent silk *sparsely* and tie off at eye.)

4 Wind on hackle 'Palmerwise' (i.e., in open turns) over body and tie off behind eye. Remove surplus hackle.

5 Pull P.V.C. slip forward and down tightly over body and tie off at eye. Whip finish and varnish the whip.
Then trim hackle fibres from *sides of body only*.

Richard Walker's Shrimp pattern has fine lead strips laid as a hump along the top of the shank under an olive wool body. This turns the fly upside down to swim more naturally. It has no upper body cover but the wool along the back is well varnished. A 'palmered' ginger hackle is used, trimmed as for The Shrimper.

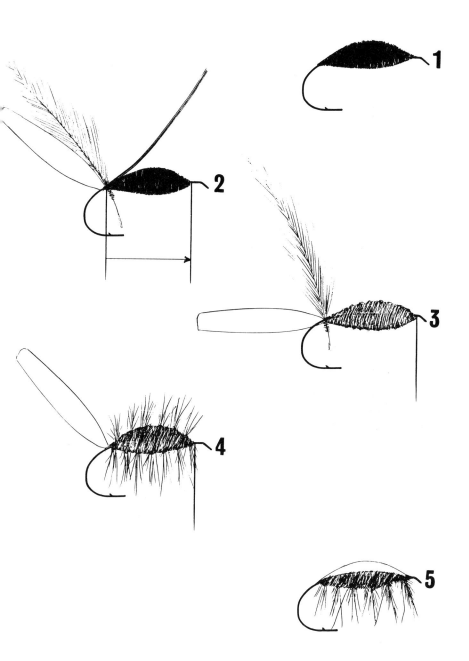

Appetiser (Bob Church)

Materials

Hook   Long shank, down eye, size 6
Working Silk   Black
*Tail   A spray of dark green cock hackle fibres and silver
mallard breast fibres, mixed*
Body   White chenille
Body Rib   Fine oval silver tinsel
*Beard Hackle   Fibres from dark green and orange hackles and
silver mallard breast feather, equal amounts, mixed*
*Wing   A generous spray of white marabou herl overlaid with
a bunch of natural grey squirrel tail hairs*
Head   Built up with working silk, green bead eyes added

Tying Instructions

1 Wind on working silk from behind eye to start of hook bend.

2 Tear out the green hackle and silver mallard breast fibres,
mix them and tie them in so that they extend approximately
$\frac{5}{16}$'' beyond bend.

3 At the same point where the tail was added, tie in the tinsel
and the chenille, in that order. Then wind working silk to ⅛''
from eye.

4 Wind on the chenille in close, firm turns to where silk hangs.
Tie off and remove surplus chenille.

5 Wind on the tinsel in open turns to end of chenille body.
Tie off and trim surplus.

6 Turn fly upside down in vice. Tear out and mix the fibres
described for beard hackle and tie these in as shown in
drawing. Trim surplus ends obscuring eye.

7 Turn fly right way up in vice. Select and tie in a generous
spray of white marabou herl to reach just short of end of
tail. Trim any excess over eye.

8 Cut squirrel tail fibres of appropriate length. Hold the
natural points in the left hand and flick out the loose shorter
hairs. Then tie in those of even length so that they reach just
short of tail end. Trim excess over eye. Varnish hair roots.

9 Build up and whip finish the head with working silk and then
tie in a green bead 'eye' on each side. Varnish head to
complete the fly. It works equally well minus eyes.

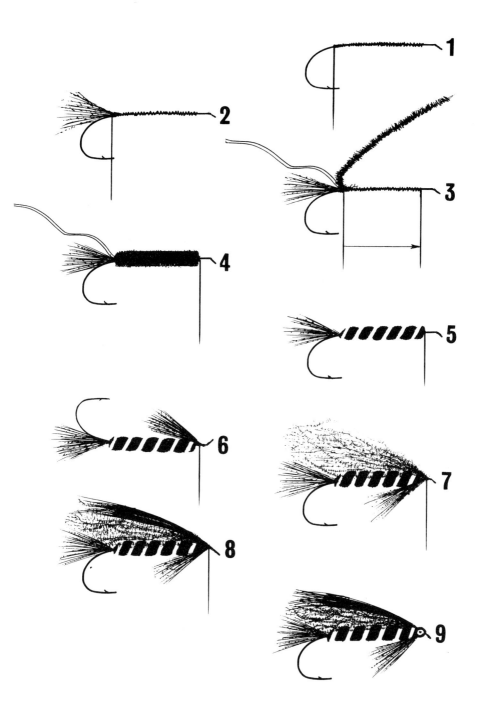

Baby Doll (Brian Kench)

Materials
Hook   Long shank, down eye, sizes 10, 8 or 6
Working Silk   Black
Body and Tail   White nylon baby wool

Tying Instructions
1 Wind on a few turns of working silk at start of bend. Cut two lengths of baby wool—one 4" the other 6" long. Fold both lengths in two centrally and tie these in *securely* where shown, leaving two loops overhanging hook bend. Then press all four strands of wool away to the left to enable you to wind the working silk in close turns round hook shank until ⅛" from eye.

2 Segregate the two longest strands of wool and wind on both together in close turns to where silk hangs. Tie off and remove surplus wool ends over eye.

3 The remaining two shorter strands of wool which were secured at bend are now pulled directly over the body and tied down securely at eye. Trim surplus wool over eye.

4 Cut centrally the two loops which overhang hook bend and fray these out for tail.

5 Wind a neat head with working silk behind hook eye, complete with a whip finish and varnish both head and whip.

Note
The hook to be used should be varnished twice to avoid staining of the wool by iron mould.

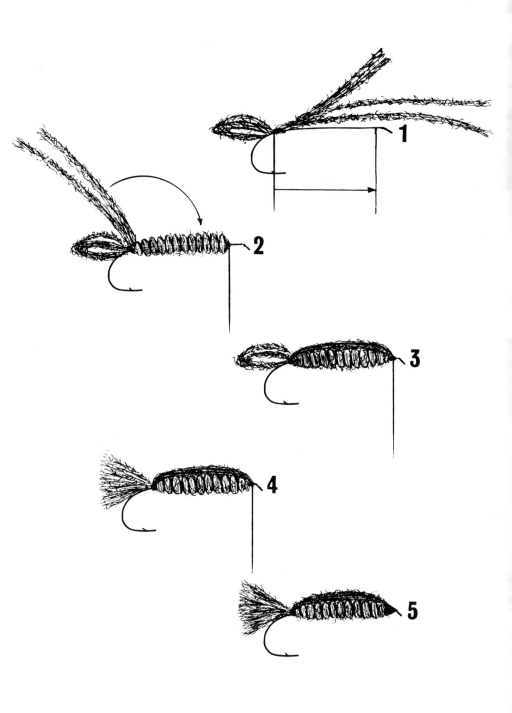

Bedhoppers (Freddie Rice)

Materials

Hook   Long shank, down eye, size 10, 8 or 6
Working Silk   Black
Tail   A spray of turkey marabou fibres   } *Colour*
Body   Chenille   } *as*
Rear Wing Overlay   A spray of turkey marabou fibres } *listed*
Front Wing Overlay   A spray of turkey marabou fibres } *below*
Head Weight   Fine lead wire
Head   Chenille as list below

Tying Instructions

1 Wind on working silk in close turns from eye to start of bend, at which point tie in tail (to extend a hook length beyond bend) and body chenille. Then wind working silk to point indicated.

2 Varnish the turns of silk and wind on the chenille in close turns to where silk hangs. Secure chenille there leaving balance for use in Operation 4.

3 Tie in rear wing overlay to extend half-way to tail tip. Then wind working silk to next point indicated.

4 Varnish the turns of silk and wind on balance of chenille to where silk hangs. Tie off and trim surplus chenille.

5 Tie in front wing overlay to reach just beyond hook bend, secure.

6 Tie in 2" chenille for head, and lead wire. Then wind working silk to just short of eye.

7 Wind on lead wire in three reducing layers to form a slight hump at head which is then varnished.

8 Wind on chenille head, whip finish and varnish the whip.

9 When wet the fly appears thus. A 6 lb. (minimum) leader is needed to fish the fly, sink and draw, to hop the lake bed, as indicated in A to A.

COLOUR COMBINATIONS

Tail	Body	Rear Overlay	Front Overlay	Head
White	White	White	Olive	Black
White	Grey	Black	Orange	White
Black	Scarlet	White	White	Black

66

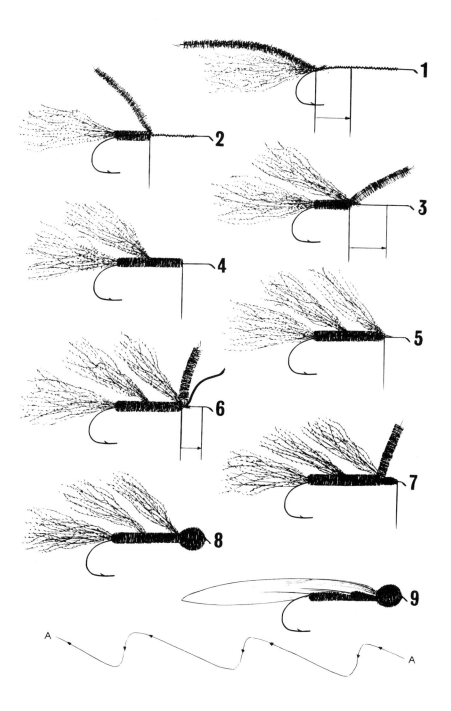

Black Chenille (Bob Church)

Materials

Hook   Long shank, down eye, size 8 or 6
Working Silk   Black
Tail   Black hackle fibres (10 to 15) or a hackle tip
Body   Black chenille
Body Rib   Silver tinsel, medium width
Beard Hackle   Black hackle fibres (approximately 15)
Wings   Four black hackles of even size

Tying Instructions

1 Wind on working silk in close turns from ⅛″ from eye to start of bend.

2 Tie in tail fibres **on top** of hook shank. Trim excess.

3 Tie in silver tinsel where tail fibres join shank. Strip ¼″ from end of chenille and tie this in at the same point, stripped end pointing to eye. Then wind working silk to ⅛″ from eye, tying down stripped end of chenille.

4 Wind on chenille closely and evenly down the shank to where the silk hangs. Tie off and trim surplus chenille.

5 Wind on silver tinsel tightly but in *open* turns to eye end of body. Tie off and trim surplus tinsel.

6 Turn fly upside down in vice. Tear approximately 15 fibres from a fairly large black hackle and tie these in as a 'beard' as shown. Trim surplus ends to clear hook eye. Then turn fly over to original position.

7 Select four black hackles judging size from illustration. These are then placed two on one side, two on the other, back to back. With these in the left hand, place them over the fly body and tie in at eye so that they lie as illustrated. Then wind a neat head, add a whip finish and varnish the head, wing roots and whipping.

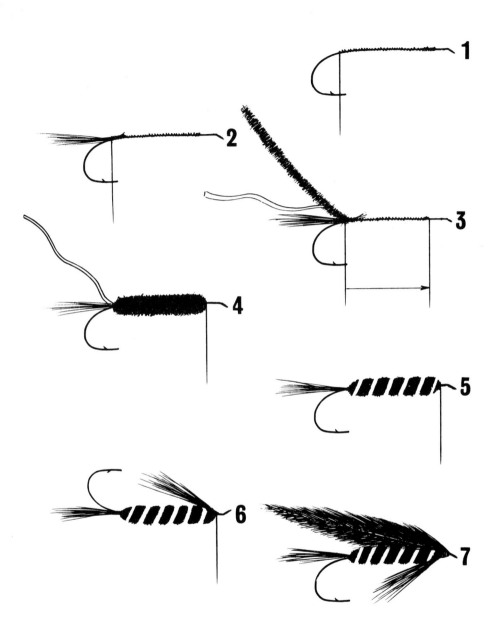

Butcher (Traditional)
Originally 'Moon's Fly'

Materials

Hook   Wide gape, down eye, size 14 to 10 (8 for sea trout)
Working Silk   Black
Tail   Three red ibis fibres or goose substitute
Body   Flat silver tinsel
Body Rib   Oval silver tinsel
Beard Hackle   Black hen (red for 'Bloody Butcher')
Wing   Paired slips from mallard blue wing quills

Tying Instructions

1 Wind on a few turns of working silk at bend and tie in tail, oval tinsel and flat tinsel in that order. Then wind working silk to ⅛" from eye in close, tight turns.

2 Coat back of flat tinsel with varnish and wind on — edge to edge — to ⅛" from eye. Tie off with working silk and remove surplus flat tinsel.

3 Wind on oval tinsel in an open spiral *the reverse way* until ⅛" from eye. Tie off with working silk and remove surplus oval tinsel, then tie in the hen hackle.

4 Wind on the hackle three or four turns towards eye. Tie off and trim surplus hackle ends.

5 Select and cut 'left' and 'right' slips of *all blue* fibres from appropriate wing quills and tie these in at eye, using the waxed loop method shown. Judge wing length from illustration. Then trim surplus wing ends neatly at eye.

6 Add a whip finish and varnish the whip.

Nowadays, the oval tinsel is largely omitted. Instead, flat tinsel is wound from behind eye to bend and then back to eye, thus forming a double layer.

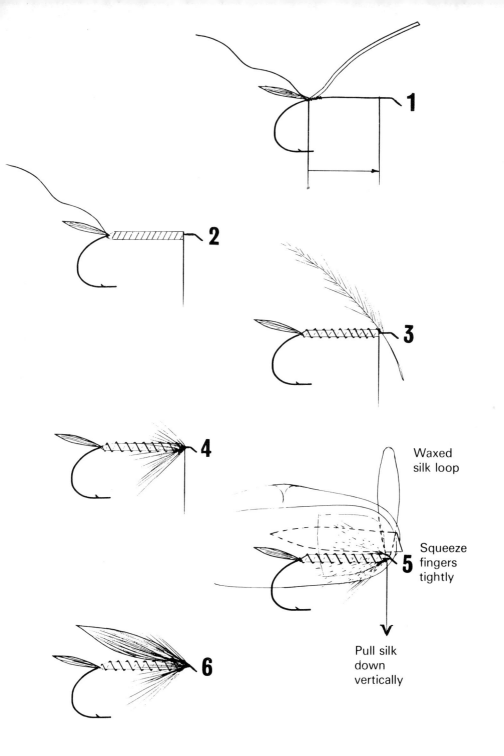

1

2

3

4

5 Waxed silk loop

Squeeze fingers tightly

Pull silk down vertically

6

Church Fry (Bob Church)

Materials

Hook   Long shank, down eye, size 10, 8, 6 or 4
Working Silk   Black
Body   Orange floss silk
Body Rib   Flat silver tinsel or lurex
Throat   Magenta fluorescent floss or silk (orange is also good)
Throat Hackle   Orange hackle fibres (15 to 20)
Wing   Natural white tipped squirrel tail hairs (20 to 30)

Tying Instructions

1 Wind on working silk from behind eye to start of bend. Tie in tinsel, then wind working silk back along two-thirds of hook shank.

2 Where silk hangs, tie in the floss silk.

3 Wind the floss evenly down the shank and back again, forming a slightly tapered body or a level body as was the original. Tie off and trim surplus floss.

4 Wind the tinsel in even, open turns to where silk hangs. Tie off and trim surplus tinsel.

5 Tie in the fluorescent floss at eye end of body.

6 Wind a 'collar' of fluorescent floss at eye end of body ⅛'' to ¼'' wide, depending on hook size.

7 Turn the fly upside down in vice. Tear out the orange hackle fibres of appropriate length and tie these in as shown in Drawing 7. Trim any hackle ends obscuring eye.

8 Turn the fly right way up in vice. Select the squirrel tail hairs, even up the white tips and tie these in *on top* of the shank so that the tips overhang bend by approximately ¼''. When they are securely tied in place, lift them and take three turns of working silk round the hair roots only to lock them in position.

9 Wind a firm but neat head ending with a whip finish and varnish the head and whip.

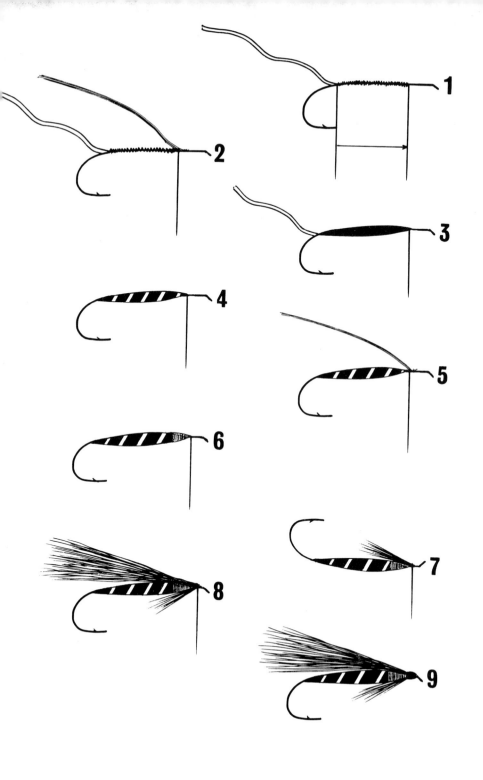

Dawn and Dusk Lure (Freddie Rice)

Materials

Hook   Long shank, fine wire, down eye, size 10, 8 or 6
Working Silk   Black
Underbody Weight   Fine lead wire (if not required, omit
Operation No. 1)
Body   Black floss
Overbody and Tail   Black squirrel tail hair surrounding body

Tying Instructions

1 Wind on lead wire from well behind eye to just short of start of bend, to form shape shown.

2 Tie in working silk at start of bend, apply two half-hitches and cut, leaving 10" hanging. Retie working silk on eye side of underbody and then tie in approximately 10" of black floss for size 6 hook, less for smaller sizes.

3 Wind black floss back and forth forming body shape ending at eye. Tie off with working silk and trim any excess floss.

4 Select the squirrel tail hairs of appropriate length and tie these in behind eye to surround the floss body. Tie off securely and trim any squirrel ends obscuring hook eye.

5 Build up a neat head at eye finishing with a whip, which should then be varnished. Allow to dry before proceeding with Operation No. 6.

6 Close the squirrel tail ends around the hook with the left hand and, pulling them firmly to the left, use the right hand to secure them in position with the working silk hanging at bend. Finish with a whip, then varnish the whole of the body, but not the tail.

Note

In the smallest size, and with a *short* body, this fly will provide a passable tadpole, which has proved a good taker in May.

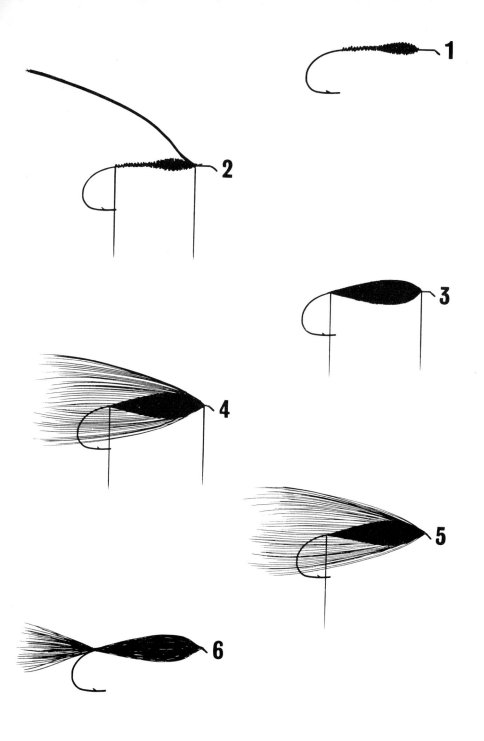

Doddlers (Freddie Rice)

Materials

Hook   Low water salmon iron, size 4, 3 or 2
Working Silk   Black

COLOUR COMBINATIONS

Tail	Body	Body Rib	Beard	Underwing	Overwing
(Squirrel)	(Chenille)	(Tinsel)	(Squirrel)	(Marabou)	(Marabou)
Scarlet	White	Silver	Olive	White	Black
Orange	Black	Gold	Black	White	Olive
Green	Grey	Silver	Orange	White	Black
Natural	White	Silver	Scarlet	White	Olive

Tying Instructions

1 Wind on working silk from behind eye to point shown where the tail, tinsel and chenille, in that order, are tied in. Wind working silk back to $\frac{3}{16}''$ from eye.

2 Varnish the shank and whilst wet wind on the chenille in close, tight turns to where silk hangs. Secure chenille with working silk and trim surplus chenille.

3 Wind on tinsel in 4 or 5 open turns to where silk hangs. Tie off and trim surplus tinsel.

4 Turn fly upside down in vice and tie in the beard fibres to length indicated. Tie off, trim any ends obscuring eye and varnish the joint.

5 Turn fly right way up in vice. Select and tie in underwing on *top* of shank to reach just short of tip of tail.

6 Select and tie in the overwing to reach just short of tip of underwing. Tie off, build up a neat head tapering to eye and varnish head three coats.

This fly is intended to winkle out bigger fish, particularly brownies, in deep areas of reservoirs and lakes. It is a fairly heavy fly and with a sinking line and a leader of adequate strength to set the hook, produces best results with a slow but *uniform* retrieve, hence the name.

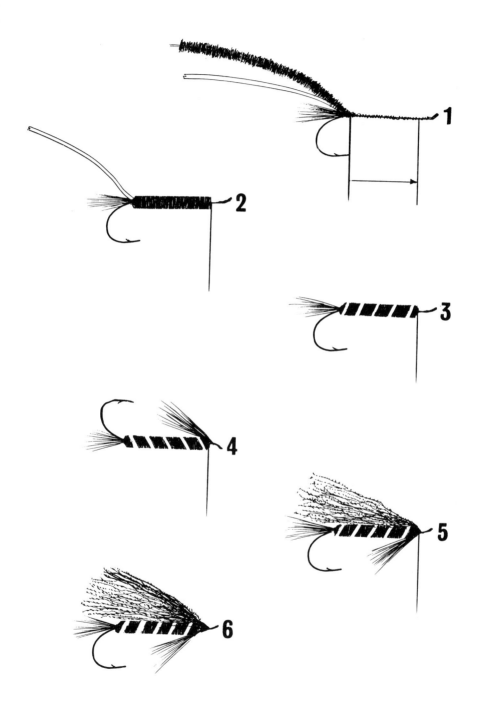

'Easytied' Trout Snacks (Freddie Rice)

Materials

Hook   Long shank, down eye, 10, 8 or 6
Working Silk   Black
Tail and Body   Rayon or silk floss (see below for colours)
Body Rib   Fine or wide silver or gold tinsel or 'Goldfingering'
used for knitting, at your choice
Beard Hackle   Cock or hen hackle fibres (see below for
colours)
Wing   Squirrel tail—natural or dyed (see below for colours)

Tying Instructions

1 Wind on a few turns of working silk at bend and tie in floss (folded twice to form tail loop) and tinsel. Then wind silk back to ⅛" from eye.

2 Wind on floss to form a flat, even body and tie off ⅛" from eye with working silk. Remove excess floss. Cut the 'loop' of floss forming tail.

3 Coat back of tinsel with varnish and wind it on in a tight even spiral to ⅛" from eye. Tie off with working silk and remove surplus tinsel.

4 Tear out a bunch of fibres from the hackle selected and tie these in as a 'beard' as shown. Tie off with working silk and remove surplus hackle ends.

5 Select about 20 or so squirrel tail fibres of chosen colour and tie these in to lie as in Drawing 5. Add a whip finish and varnish the whip and wing roots.

COLOUR COMBINATIONS

Tail and Body	Beard Hackle	Squirrel Tail Wing
Black	Red	Hot orange
Scarlet	Black	Black or natural
Hot orange	Red	Black or natural
Yellow	Hot orange	Brown
Green	Black	Black or hot orange

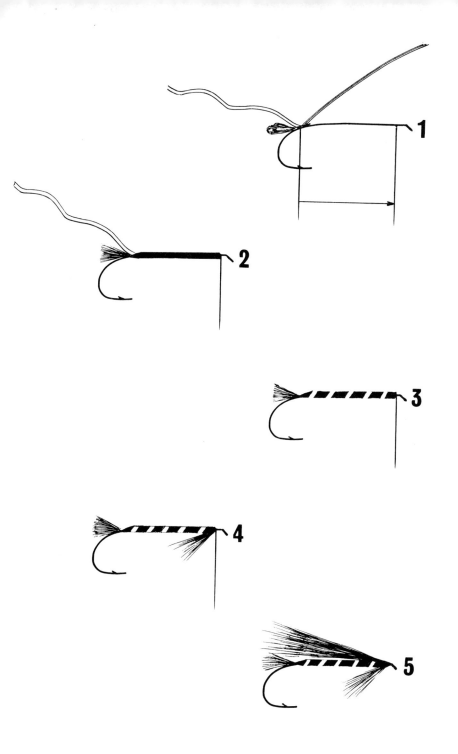

Epsom Salt (Freddie Rice)

Materials

Hook   Long shank, down eye, size 6, 8 or 10
Working Silk   Hot orange
Body (Rear two-thirds)   Medium green or natural seal fur
Body (Front one-third)   Red and orange seal fur mixed
Body Rib   Silver wire
Tail and Overbody   5 to 8 natural peacock herls
Head Hackle   Hot orange cock hackle

Tying Instructions

1 Wind on a few turns of working silk at start of hook bend then tie in peacock herls (leaving good ¼" protruding for tail) and silver wire.

2 Coat working silk with liquid wax and dub on green seal fur.

3 Wind on dubbed seal fur to form rear two-thirds of body.

4 Change dubbing to the mixed red and orange seal fur, waxing a further length of working silk if necessary.

5 Wind this on to form front one-third of body.

6 Pick up the silver wire and wind this on tightly in an open spiral to head. Tie off with working silk *or* take two full turns of wire round hook shank. Trim surplus wire.

7 Pull down the peacock herls over the whole body and tie these down at head. Trim surplus herls.

8 Select a hot orange cock hackle of appropriate size. Strip the lower third and tie this in at head.

9 Wind on the hackle (using hackle pliers or fingers) 2 or 3 turns only to form a 'collar' as shown. Trim waste, add a whip finish and varnish the whip.

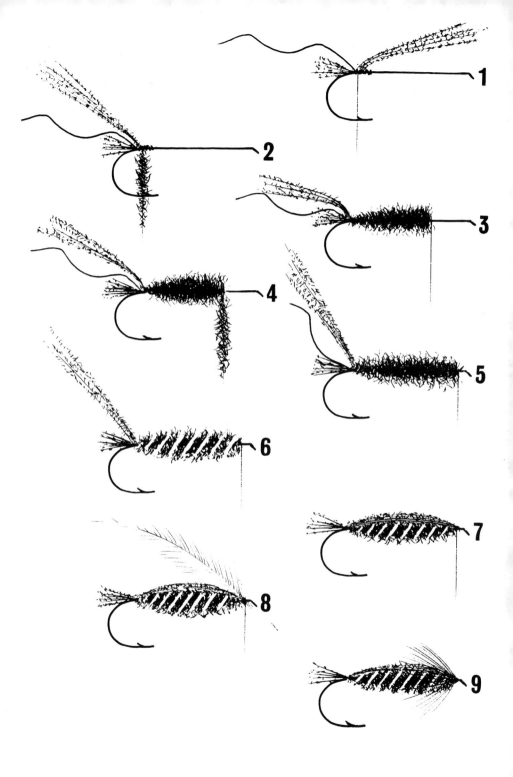

'G.J.' Fingerling (Freddie Rice)

Materials

Hook   Long shank, down eye, fine wire, size 6 or 8
Working Silk   Hot orange
Tail and Overbody   Five peacock herls, bronze
Underbody   White floss
Body Cover   Silver or gold Mylar tubing — medium
Beard Hackle   Hot orange hackle fibres
Head   Fluorescent floss, scarlet

Tying Instructions

1 Wind on a few turns of working silk at bend then tie in the peacock herls (to extend ¼" or so beyond start of bend) and approximately 6" to 8" floss. Tie two half-hitches and then cut working silk to leave 6" hanging free. Retie fresh silk ³⁄₁₆" from eye and cut leaving 9".

2 Wind on floss forming body shape as you go. Tie off with two turns and remove waste floss.

3 Cut a piece of Mylar tubing of appropriate size and extract core. Feed Mylar tube over silk and hook eye and press to meet tail. Use silk hanging at bend to secure Mylar and add whip. Trim waste silk at bend. Secure Mylar at eye end with hanging silk.

4 Varnish body and whilst still wet pull down peacock herls over body and secure at eye with working silk.

5 Turn fly upside down in vice. Select a small bunch of hot orange hackle fibres and tie these in as shown. Trim waste fibre ends.

6 Tie in 3" scarlet fluorescent floss behind head end of body then wind working silk to just behind eye.

7 Wind on fluorescent floss to form a substantial head shaped as shown. Tie off, add a whip finish and varnish whip.

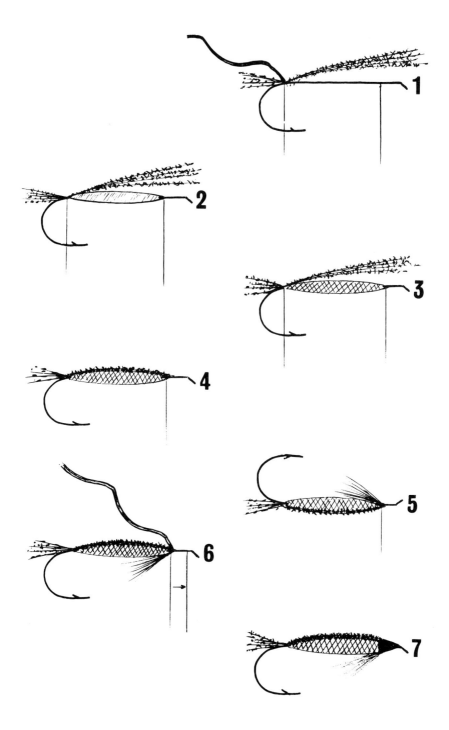

Grey and Red Matuka (Dave Collyer)

Materials

Hook   Standard or long shank, down eye, size 6
Working Silk   White or grey
Body   Silver-grey chenille
Body Rib   Oval silver tinsel
Beard Hackle   Scarlet hackle fibres
Wing   Two round-ended white/brown hen pheasant flank
feathers

Tying Instructions

1 Wind on a few turns of working silk at bend, and tie in
chenille and oval silver tinsel. Then wind working silk back in
close turns to *at least* ⅛'' from eye.

2 Wind on chenille to form body and tie off leaving room for
beard hackle and wing. Remove surplus chenille.

3 Turn hook upside down in vice. Tear out a bunch of fibres of
appropriate length from a scarlet hackle and tie these in as
shown.

4 Prepare two white/brown hen pheasant flank feathers so
that each results as Drawing 4.

5 Turn hook right way up in vice. Tie in the hen pheasant flank
feathers back to back at head with stripped side of quills
lying over hook shank. Then wind the tinsel through the
fibres and over hook shank, parting the fibres with a dubbing
needle as you go to prevent them from being caught and
flattened. Tie off and remove surplus tinsel.

6 Slope fibres towards tail, whip finish and varnish the whip.

A variation, using badger saddle hackles, natural or dyed red
or hot orange, coupled with white chenille body, is also
good.

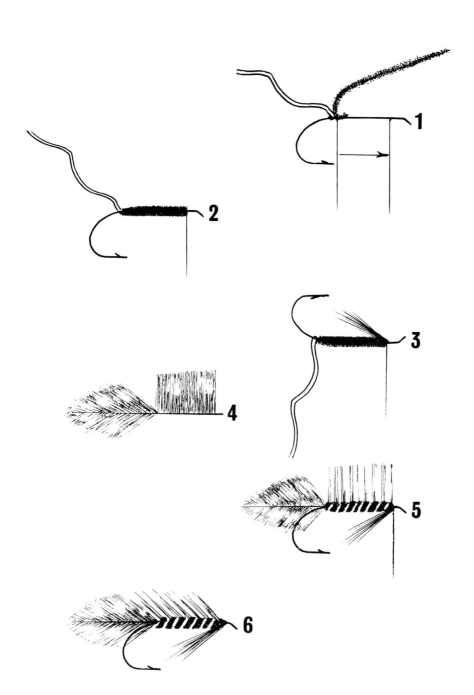

Hot Pants (Freddie Rice)

Materials

Hook Standard or long shank, size 10 or 8
Working Silk Black
Weighted Underbody One layer finest lead wire or two layers of copper wire
Tag (or Pants) Fluorescent hot-orange nylon floss
Body Four strands peacock herl (black chenille for substitute)
Wing 10-15 squirrel tail fibres dyed hot-orange
Hackle 3-4 turns of a long fibred black hen hackle

Tying Instructions

1 Wind on the fine lead (or copper) wire in close turns as specified above until layers completed. *Press in the final end.*

2 Wind on a few turns of working silk partly round hook bend and tie in fluorescent floss. Then wind silk ⅛" toward eye.

3 With the working silk left hanging, wind on the floss back and forth over approximately ⅛" to form the tag finishing at the rear end of the underbody. Tie off with working silk and trim surplus floss.

4 Tie in four strands of peacock herl at eye end of tag.

5 Varnish the underbody and whilst it is still wet, twist the peacock herls into a 'rope' and wind the 'rope' over the underbody until ⅛" from hook eye. The peacock ends are then temporarily secured in hackle pliers.

6 Keeping the working silk *taut,* wind this in open turns to eye end of body, at which point the peacock ends are tied in and excess herl trimmed.

7 Select the squirrel tail fibres and laying these over body so that fine tips extend just beyond tag, tie them in with working silk. Varnish these tyings and trim, diagonally, the squirrel ends obscuring hook eye.

8 Select the hen hackle described and tie this in as shown.

9 Wind on the hen hackle—three to four turns and tie off with working silk. Trim surplus hackle, add a whip finish and varnish the whip.

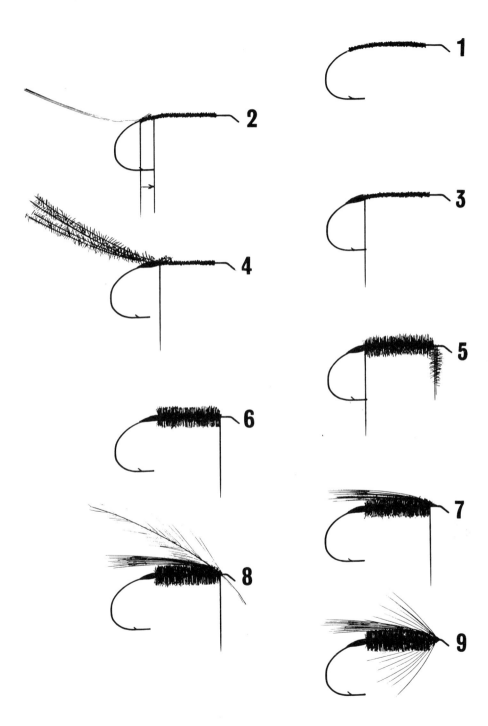

Jersey Herd (Tom Ivens)

Materials

Hook Long shank, down eye, size 8 or 6
Working Silk Black or hot orange
Underbody White floss silk
Body Cover Wide copper coloured tinsel or milk cap foil,
 gold lurex or tinsel as substitute
Tail and Overbody 8 to 12 strands natural peacock herl
Hackle Hot orange dyed cock hackle
Head Twisted peacock herl

Tying Instructions

1 Wind on a few turns of working silk at bend and tie in
  peacock herls (leaving $5/16$" or so projecting for the tail), the
  tinsel and floss silk in that order. Then wind on working silk
  to $3/16$" from eye.

2 Wind on floss silk, thickening at centre until $3/16$" from eye.
  Tie off and remove surplus floss silk.

3 Coat back of tinsel with varnish and wind on tightly, leaving
  no gaps, until $3/16$" from eye. Tie off using working silk and
  remove surplus tinsel.

4 Coat upper edge of body with varnish and whilst wet pull
  peacock herl down and forward, pressing it on to varnish.
  Tie herl down $3/16$" from eye with working silk. **Do not** remove
  surplus herl.

5 Select and tie in with working silk a single short fibred cock
  hackle dyed hot orange at eye end of body.

6 Wind on hackle (doubled) for two full turns only. Tie off with
  working silk and remove surplus hackle ends.

7 Twist peacock herl ends together and wind these on two
  turns to form a neat head. Tie off with working silk and
  remove any herl ends remaining. Add a whip finish and
  varnish the whip.

Note

For a leaded version tie in and wind on lead in Operation 1
before winding on floss silk underbody.

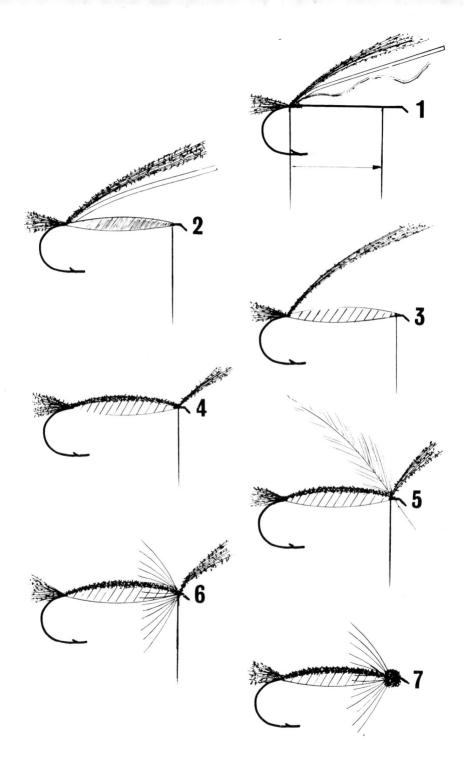

Long John Silver (Freddie Rice)

Materials

Hook   Standard or long shank, down eye, size 8
Working Silk   White
Tail   4 white or black, plus 2 olive, ostrich herls, mixed
Rear Body   Scarlet chenille
Front Body   Black chenille
Front Body Rib   Medium width silver tinsel or lurex

Tying Instructions

1 Wind on working silk from behind eye to start of bend at which point the mixed ostrich herls are tied in so that they overhang hook bend by 1¾".

2 Strip ³⁄₁₆" from the scarlet chenille and tie in at bend, core towards eye. Then wind working silk over two-thirds of hook length, covering the ostrich core.

3 Wind on scarlet chenille in close tight turns to where working silk hangs and tie off. Trim excess chenille.

4 Tie in silver tinsel. Then wind working silk to just short of eye.

5 Strip ³⁄₁₆" from the black chenille and tie this in with stripped core pointing towards bend.

6 Wind on the black chenille until it is right up to the scarlet portion of body, then back over those turns until just short of eye, thus providing a form of enlarged head. Tie off and trim surplus chenille.

7 Wind on silver tinsel in three open turns to eye. Tie off and trim surplus tinsel. Then wind a neat head, complete with a whip finish and varnish the whip.

Note

Weight can be added prior to operation 1. Use lead wire, closely wound from eye to bend.

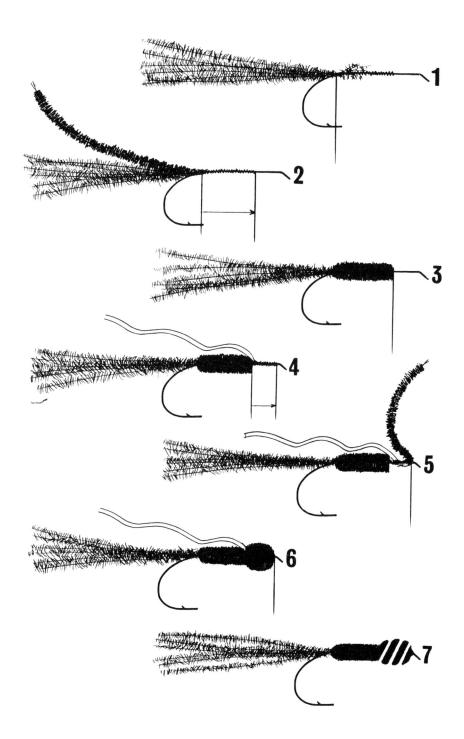

Long Tailed Tit

Materials

Hook   Down eye, size 10 or 8
Working Silk   Black
Underbody   Fine lead or copper wire
Body   3 strands peacock herl (Green/bronze)
Tails   4 strands peacock herl (Green/bronze) extending 1½''
*   to 2'' beyond bend*
Beard   6 to 10 white hackle fibres

Tying Instructions

1 Wind on lead or copper wire in close turns from ⅛'' behind
  eye to start of hook bend, thickening in the centre.

2 Wind on a few turns of working silk at eye then tie in
  three peacock herls for body and four similar herls for tails to
  extend 1½'' to 2'' beyond bend.

3 Wind working silk over tails and lead underbody, ending at
  rear of body. Then varnish the underbody.

4 *Whilst the underbody is still wet,* twist the three body herls
  into a 'rope' and wind this on in close turns to rear of
  underbody. Tie off and remove surplus body herl ends
  leaving tail herls untouched.

5 Keeping the working silk taut, wind this over body in wide,
  open turns to hook eye. Then tie in the beard fibres to
  project toward hook point. A neat head is then formed
  ending with a whip finish which is then varnished.

Note

Notwithstanding the short hook and long tails, it will be found
that this fly is normally taken well and fish do not 'come short'.

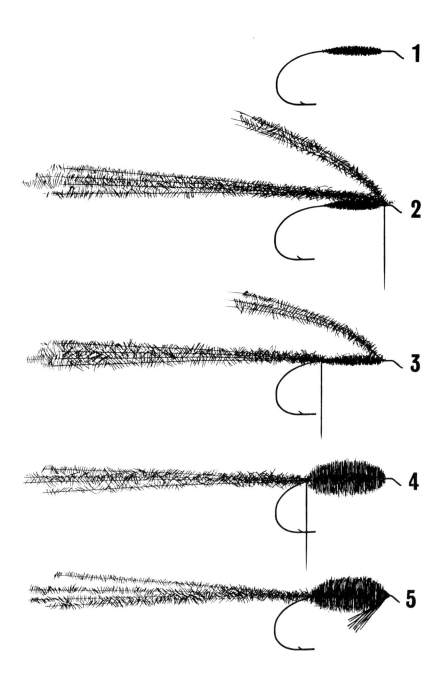

Mrs Palmer (Richard Walker)

Materials

Hook   Long shank, down eye, size 8 or 6 (old scale)
Working Silk   Black
Body   White daylight fluorescent wool from start of bend to
   ¼" from eye, then 3 or 4 turns of arc chrome fluorescent
   wool to ⅛" short of eye
Body Rib   Over white wool only—fine flat silver tinsel
Wing   Palest yellow goat hair, twice hook length
Hackle   White cock hackle fibres tied in as a beard
Cheeks   Jungle cock or substitute

Tying Instructions

1 Wind on a few turns of working silk at start of bend and tie
  in a length of white d/f wool and the silver tinsel. Then wind
  working silk to ¼" from eye.

2 Wind on white d/f wool to form a slim body ending where
  silk hangs. Trim surplus wool.

3 Wind on silver tinsel in open turns as rib. Tie off when
  working silk is reached and trim surplus tinsel.

4 Tie in a short length of arc chrome d/f wool. Then wind
  working silk ⅛" toward eye.

5 Wind on 3 or 4 turns of arc chrome wool to cover
  approximately ⅛" then tie off and trim surplus wool.

6 Tie in a bunch of palest yellow goat hairs securely. Trim any
  surplus ends extending over eye. Turn fly upside down in
  vice.

7 Tear a bunch (12 to 15) of fibres from a white hackle and
  tie these in as a beard. Trim surplus ends over eye.

8 Turn fly right way up in vice. Select two jungle cock
  feathers, or substitutes, and tie these in at head, one to lie
  along each side of wing. Wind a neat head ending with a
  whip finish and varnish both head and whipping.

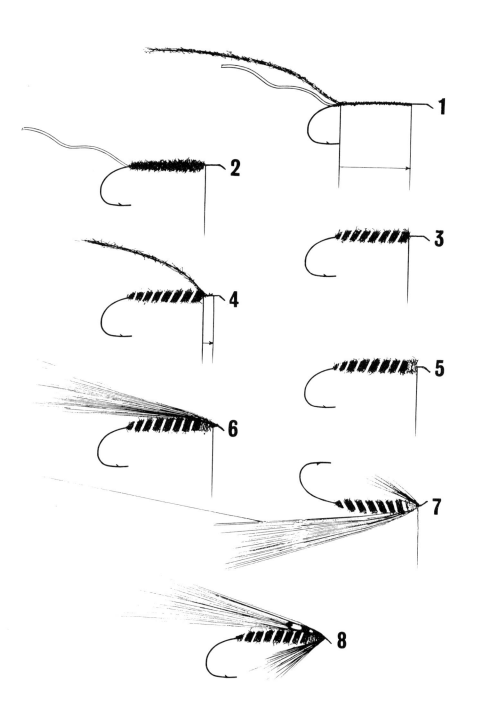

Muddler Minnow (Don Gapen, USA)

Materials

Hook   Long shank, down eye, size 4 to 6
Working Silk   Brown
Tail   Folded slip of oak turkey wing fibres
Body   Flat gold tinsel
Wing   Sandwich of oak turkey-grey squirrel-oak turkey
Hackle   Deer hair fibres
Head   Deer hair fibres 'spun' on and clipped to shape

Tying Instructions

1   Tie in several turns of working silk at bend then add a folded slip of oak turkey wing quill for tail of size appropriate to hook and flat gold tinsel. Then wind silk to within $\frac{5}{16}$'' of eye.

2   Wind on tinsel in tight *touching* turns to $\frac{5}{16}$'' from eye and tie off.

3   Select and tie in (at point where silk hangs) approximately 15 to 20 fibres from a grey squirrel tail to reach a little beyond hook bend as shown. Half-hitch with working silk to secure.

4   Select a 'left' and a 'right' slip from an oak turkey wing quill and tie these in, one on either side of the squirrel fibres, length as illustration. Some prefer a shorter wing.

4A Select a small bunch of natural deer body hairs and take two slack turns round these and hook shank as in 4A. Pulling the silk (and assisting the operation with the fingers) will result in these hairs spinning round the shank as in 4B. Several such 'spinnings' are necessary, each being pressed against the first. When spinnings are on, clip the front hair to a round 'ball' shape as shown leaving a few long hairs pointing to the rear as shown in Drawing 5. Whip finish and varnish the whip.

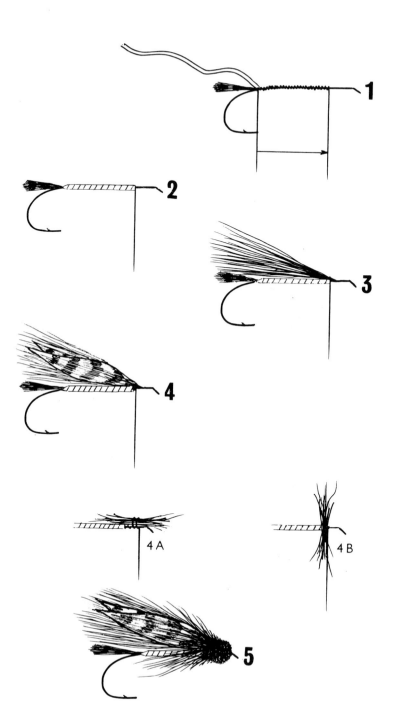

Polystickle (Richard Walker)

Materials

Hook   Long shank, down eye, 8 or 6 (8 most popular)
Working Silk   Black
Underbody   Flat silver tinsel
Gut   Fluorescent (or normal) scarlet floss or wool
Body Cover   Polythene (P.V.C.) strip stretched before winding
   on
Tail and Back   Raffene strip (³⁄₁₆'' wide) wet and pulled
   tightly to eye — brown, brown-olive, buff, yellow, orange,
   green, green-olive, at your choice
Throat   Either a slip of red wool or floss, or red hackle fibres
   tied underneath as a beard or false hackle
Head   Working silk wound on to form a substantial head

Tying Instructions

1 Wind on tight turns of working silk from eye to bend and
   then tie in underbody tinsel, P.V.C. and body cover strip and
   Raffene for tail/back, so that approximately ¼'' extends over
   bend. Then wind working silk over two-thirds of shank
   towards eye.

2 Wind on tinsel in widely spaced turns to where silk hangs.
   Tie off and remove surplus tinsel.

3 Tie in floss for 'gut', then wind working silk to ⅛'' from eye.

4 Wind on floss forming 'gut', tying off at ⅛'' from eye.

5 Wind on *stretched* P.V.C. tightly to and fro forming body
   shape ending at point where silk hangs. Tie off and remove
   surplus P.V.C. Varnish body two coats.

6 Wet Raffene, pull this *tightly* over body to eye and tie in.
   Remove surplus Raffene at eye.

7 Tie in 'throat' material (I prefer the scarlet hackle fibres)
   turning the hook upside down in the vice as this eases the
   operation. Trim off any surplus extending over eye.

8 Using your working silk wind on a substantial head as
   shown, finishing with a neat whip finish. An 'eye' can be
   added on each side of head, but this is optional.

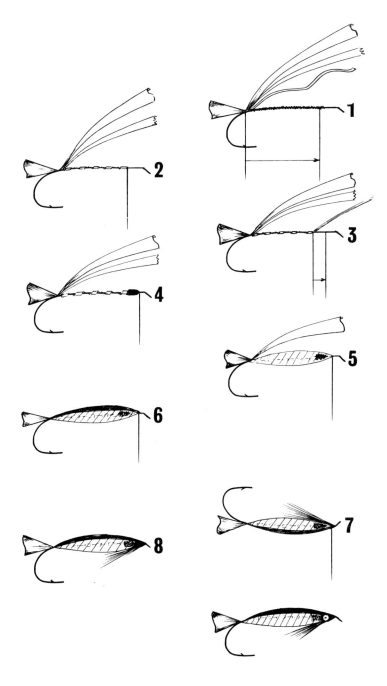

Rainbird (Freddie Rice)

Materials

Hook   Cranked shank keel hook, size 8
Working Silk   Black
Body   Black floss
Body Rib   Flat gold tinsel
Wing   Squirrel tail dyed hot orange
Rear Head   Scarlet fluorescent wool
Front Head   Peacock sword fibres

Tying Instructions

1 Wind on tight turns of working silk to bend and tie in flat tinsel and black floss. Then wind working silk to point A.

2 Wind on floss in flat even turns to point A. Tie off and remove surplus floss.

3 Wind on tinsel tightly in an open spiral and tie off. Remove surplus tinsel. Then turn hook upside down in vice.

4 Select a small bunch of squirrel tail fibres dyed hot orange and tie these in just to right of point A and add in 2" scarlet fluorescent wool.

5 Wind on fluorescent wool to form a band ⅛" wide. When tying off add in three peacock sword fibres.

6 Twist the peacock sword fibres and wind on to form a neat round head. Tie off, remove surplus peacock ends. Add a whip finish and varnish the whip.

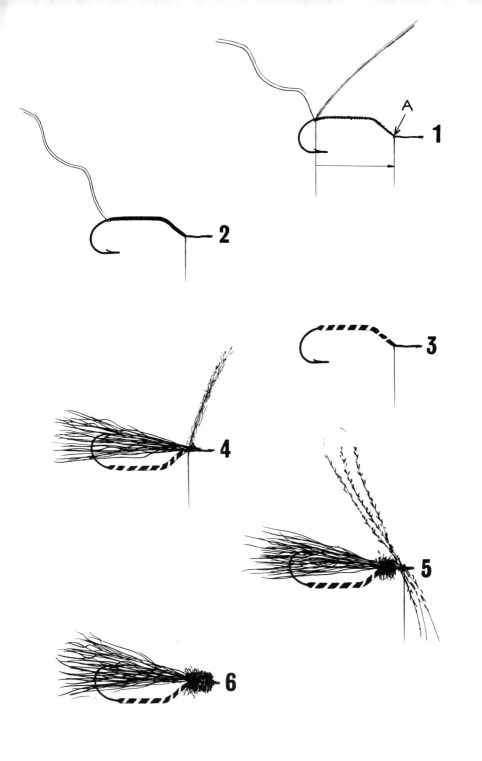

Rassler (Steve Parton)
(A buoyant fly)

Materials

Hook   Long shank, down eye, sizes 10, 8 or 6
Working Silk   Black or brown
Body   Polyethylene glued on to shank and shaped
Tail and Back   Speckled turkey fibres
Head and Fins   Deer (body) hair

Preparing the Body

A Cut a rectangle of polyethylene (size is indicated in Illustration 'C') and cut a slit lengthwise to half depth.

B Prepare the hook by winding on working silk from approx ¼'' from eye to start of bend. Let silk hang.

C Apply waterproof glue (I use 'Araldite') to the turns of silk and place a little in the slit made in the polyethylene. Push the polyethylene on to the hook shank so that the latter is firmly embedded, and set aside to dry. Prepare a number in this way on the hook sizes listed.

D When the glue has set, trim the polyethylene to a bomb shape with a very sharp knife or razor blade.

Tying Instructions

1 Select and tie in the speckled turkey fibres at bend so that a tail is formed as shown. Secure with a whip, varnish and trim off working silk. Leave turkey fibres.

2 Retie working silk at eye end. Apply waterproof glue along the ridge of the body, press the turkey fibres on to it and tie down to shank at the front.

3 Cut the deer body hair from the skin and, with the left hand, place this horizontally over shank at eye end. Take two loose turns of working silk round hair and shank.

4 Pulling the silk and assisting with the fingers will result in the hair 'spinning' round the shank. Press this close up to the fly body with an empty ball pen shell.

5 Repeat 3 and 4 until space from eye to body is almost filled with 'spinnings'. Tie off and complete with a whip finish.

6 Trim the hair to shape with scissors leaving some projecting one each **side** of the body to represent the fins of a bullhead. Varnish the whip and the speckled turkey along the back.

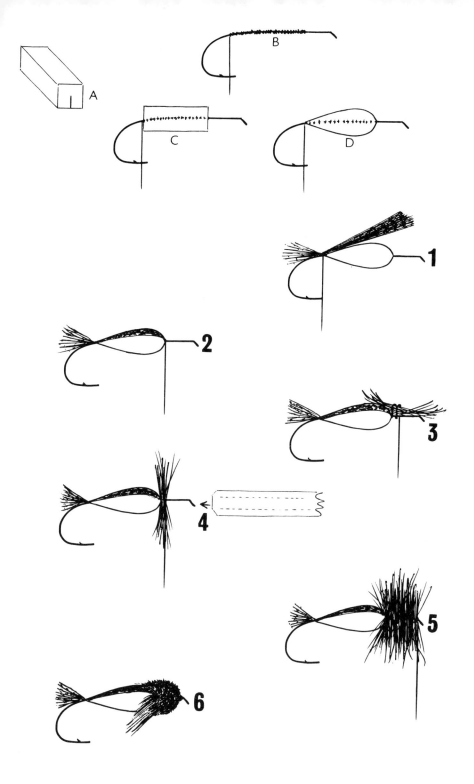

Sinfoil's Fry (Ken Sinfoil)

Materials

Hook   Long shank, fine wire, down eye, 6, 8 or 10
Working Silk   Black
Underbody   Flat silver tinsel
Overbody   Heavy gauge polythene ¹⁄₁₆'' to ⅛'' wide
Gut   Scarlet floss silk or fluorescent floss
Back   Pale brown mallard fibres

Tying Instructions

1 Wind on a few turns of working silk at start of bend. Tie in tinsel and then wind working silk back to ³⁄₁₆'' from eye.

2 Wind on tinsel in tight, touching turns until silk is reached. Tie off and remove surplus tinsel.

3 Tie in polythene strip at head.

4 Wind this polythene strip tightly back and forth forming the body shape. Tie off at eye and remove surplus polythene.

5 Tie in scarlet floss at head.

6 Wind on floss to form the 'gut'. Then varnish the whole body two coats.

7 Tear out a small bunch of fibres from the poor side of a brown mallard shoulder feather and tie these in so that they lie flat over body and just reach outside of hook bend.

8 Build up a head with working silk, add a whip finish and varnish head and whip several coats.

9 Paint an 'eye' on each side of head.

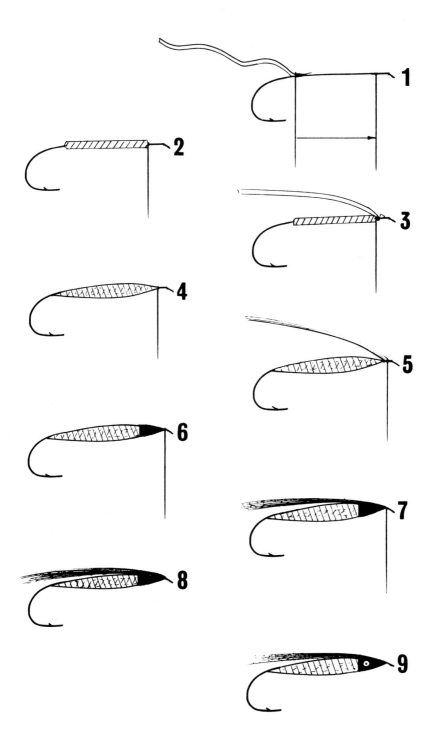

Sweeney Todd (Richard Walker)

Materials

*Hook   Long shank, down eye, standard or fine wire, size 8, 6
or 4 (6 most popular)*
Working Silk   Black
Body   Black floss
Rib   Flat silver tinsel—medium
Head   Magenta fluorescent wool
Beard Hackle   Scarlet hackle fibres (approx. 10)
Wing   Black squirrel tail (smaller sizes) or bucktail (larger sizes)

Tying Instructions

1 Wind on a few turns of working silk at start of bend then
tie in flat silver tinsel and black floss in that order.

2 Wind working silk back to ¾₆'' from eye.

3 Wind on floss silk forming body shape. Tie off at eye with
two turns of working silk. Remove surplus floss.

4 Wind on flat silver tinsel in a tight, even spiral to eye. When
tying off with working silk add in the 2'' of magenta
fluorescent wool. Wind silk to eye.

5 Wind on the magenta wool to form head as shown. Tie off
two turns.

6 *Turn fly upside down in vice.* Tear out a small bunch of fibres
from a scarlet cock hackle and tie these in as shown for a
'beard' hackle. Tie off with two turns of working silk.
Reverse hook right way up.

7 Select 15-20 black squirrel (or bucktail) hairs and tie these
in at head so that they lie *above* fly body. Well varnish the
joint of hairs to body to add to strength. Wind on working
silk to form a neat head, add a whip finish and varnish the
whip.

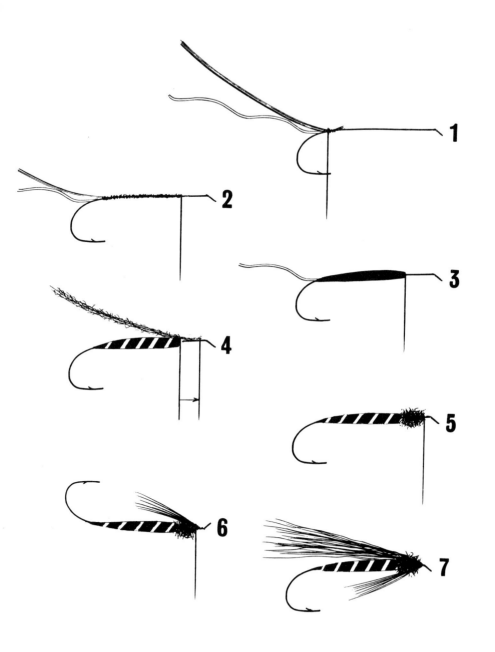

Tube Flies (Freddie Rice)

Materials

Hook   To hold tube, a NO-EYE salmon hook or bodkin
Tube   Polythene, aluminium or brass tube, ½" to 1¼", or,
for small sizes, hard nylon tube ½" to ¾", see Drawing A
Working Silk   Black
Body, Rib, Wing, Head Hackle   See list below

Tying Instructions

B Set the salmon hook or bodkin in the vice and press the tube on to it firmly.

1 Wind on a few turns of working silk at left end of tube and tie in tinsel and floss. Then wind working silk to ⅛" from right end of tube.

2 Wind on floss keeping it laid flat over tube until ⅛" from end. Tie off and remove surplus floss.

3 Wind on tinsel tightly in an open spiral to end of floss body. Tie off and remove surplus tinsel.

4 Select about 6 to 10 bucktail or squirrel hairs and tie these in as shown.

A Trim surplus ends at right.

B Turn tube 25° on hook or bodkin and repeat 4 above, keeping turns of silk moving to the right to avoid building a bulky head.

C Repeat 4B.

D Repeat 4B so that hair now surrounds the tube.

5 Tie in the selected hackle.

A Wind on the hackle using fingers or hackle pliers. Tie off, trim surplus, whip finish and varnish the whip.

6 To use the fly, feed the nylon cast through the tube and then tie in a small treble hook which, if desired, may be adorned with a small matching hackle wound on the stem as in 5B.

Body (Floss)	Rib (Tinsel)	Wing	Head Hackle
Black	Oval gold	Brown bucktail	Blue Gallena
Yellow	Flat silver	Brown squirrel	Black
Teal blue	Flat silver	Black bucktail	Badger
Scarlet	Oval gold	Natural squirrel	Hot orange

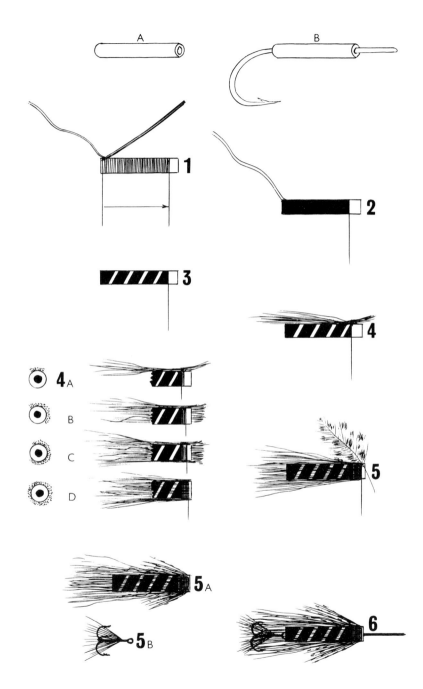

Whisky Fly (Albert Willock)

Materials

Hook   Long shank, down eye, round bend, size 8
Working Silk   None, fluorescent floss takes its place
Body   Silver (or gold) Sellotape (colour optional)
Tag   Scarlet fluorescent floss
Body Rib   Scarlet fluorescent floss
Wing   Calf tail dyed hot orange
Head Hackle   Hot orange cock hackle
Head   Longish and built up with fluorescent floss

Tying Instructions

1 This defines area to be covered with Sellotape.

2 Sellotape cut and attached to hook shank.

3 Sellotape body rolled on.

4 Tie in fluorescent floss at bend and form a tag at end of body.

5 Wind on fluorescent floss in a tight open spiral over body. Now varnish whole body two coats.

6 Select a bunch of hot orange calf tail fibres and tie these in using the floss as working silk.

7 Select a hot orange hackle of appropriate size and tie this in using the floss as working silk.

8 Wind on hackle to form a collar. Tie off using floss and remove waste hackle.

9 Using the fluorescent floss build up a longish head as shown. Add a whip finish and varnish whole head two coats.

The **Whisky Muddler** combines Whisky Fly body and wing with Muddler wing and hair head.

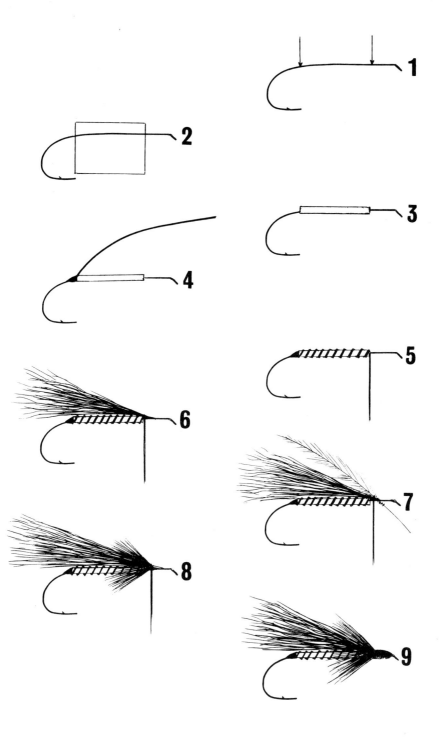

Bibliography

COLLYER, David J.	*Fly Dressing* (1975)
COURTNEY WILLIAMS, A.	*A Dictionary of Trout Flies* (1965)
GODDARD, John	*Trout Fly Recognition* (1966) *Trout Flies of Stillwater* (1969)
IVENS, T. C.	*Stillwater Fly Fishing* (1961)
LAWRIE, W. H.	*International Trout Flies* (1969)
LEONARD, J. Edson	*Flies* (1960)
PRICE, S. D. (Taff)	*Lures for Game, Coarse and Sea Fishing* (1972)
SAWYER, Frank	*Nymphs and the Trout* (1970)
VENIARD, John	*Fly Dressers' Guide* (1952) *Reservoir and Lake Flies* (1970)

Periodicals

Angling	Monthly
Angling Times	Weekly
Trout and Salmon	Monthly